Sympathetic Seeing

Sympathetic Seeing:

Esther McCoy and the Heart of American Modernist Architecture and Design

Written and edited by Kimberli Meyer and Susan Morgan

Published with the assistance of the Getty Foundation, the National Endowment for the Arts, the Graham Foundation, the Los Angeles County Arts Commission, and the City of West Hollywood Arts and Cultural Affairs Commission

This book was published on the occasion of the exhibition
Sympathetic Seeing: Esther McCoy and the Heart of American Modernist Architecture and Design, organized by the MAK Center for Art and Architecture, Los Angeles, at the Schindler House, September 28, 2011–January 8, 2012.

Curators: Kimberli Meyer and Susan Morgan
Editors/Authors: Kimberli Meyer, Susan Morgan
Editorial Assistance: Anthony Carfello, Priscilla Chung
Copy Editing: Elizabeth Pulsinelli
Book Design: Roman Jaster

MAK Center for Art and Architecture, Los Angeles
at the Schindler House
835 North Kings Road
West Hollywood, CA 90069
USA
Tel. (323) 651-1510
Fax (323) 651-2340
office@MAKcenter.org
www.MAKcenter.org

Verlag für moderne Kunst Nürnberg
Königstraße 73
90402 Nürnberg
Tel. (+49 911) 23 73 100-0
Fax (+49 911) 23 73 100-99
verlag@moderne-kunst.org
www.vfmk.de

ISBN: 978-3-86984-265-3

This publication is made possible in part by the Austrian Federal Ministry for Education, Arts and Culture.

D.A.P. / Distributed Art Publishers, Inc.
155 Sixth Avenue, 2nd Floor
New York, NY 10013
USA
Tel. (212) 627-1999
Fax (212) 627-9484
www.artbook.com

Distributed in the United Kingdom:
Cornerhouse Publications
70 Oxford Street, Manchester M1 5 NH, UK
Tel. (+44-161) 200 15 03
Fax (+44-161) 200 15 04

Distributed in Europe (except UK):
LKG Leipziger Kommissions- und
Buchhandelsgesellschaft mbH
Tel. (+49 34026) 65107
Fax (+49 34026) 651732
ekaiser@lkg-service.de

Set in Fairfield (1939) by Rudolf Ruzicka
and Avenir (1988) by Adrian Frutiger

Printed by Paper Chase Printing in California, USA
First Edition: 1,600

Acknowledgements

With a historical project like *Sympathetic Seeing*, primary research is essential. For funding provided to Susan Morgan in order to conduct research into the life and work of Esther McCoy, we are grateful to the Graham Foundation for the Advanced Studies in the Fine Arts, the Beverly Willis Architecture Foundation, and the Smithsonian Institution for their crucial support. Special thanks to Sarah Herda, Beverly Willis, and Wanda Bubriski for their commitment to recognizing women in architecture, and to Liza Kirwin, curator of manuscripts at the Archives of American Art, for her erudite navigational skills of the Smithsonian. McCoy was a prolific writer and indefatigable researcher, and the AAA's McCoy collection provides a personal and panoramic view of the American twentieth century. For excellent guidance and assistance with collections, thanks to Marisa Bourgoin, chief of reference services at the AAA; writer Darcy Tell, editor of the Archives of American Art Journal; audio-visual archivist Megan McShea; and Wendy Hurlock Baker, Elizabeth Botten, Jen Dismukes, Susan Cary, Erin Corley Kinhart, and John W. Smith. For their support of independent scholarship, thanks to Sam Albert, Nelson Aldrich, Julie Ault, Alix Browne, Jocelyn Gibbs, Fritz Haeg, Brooke Hodge, Shirley Irons, Bill Irvine, Tom Lawson, Judy Linn, Diana Murphy, Maureen Selwood, Howard Singerman, Elizabeth A.T. Smith, and Diana Stoll. Thanks to McCoy's friend Joseph Giovannini for his well-informed and sympathetic support, and to McCoy's friends and associates Diana Balmori, Baylis Glascock, Peter Kirby, Kathryn Metz, Andy Spence, David Travers, and Robert Winter for providing both information and insight.

The exhibition at the Schindler House was made possible by funding from the National Endowment for the Arts, the Graham Foundation, the Los Angeles County Arts Commission, and the City of West Hollywood Arts and Cultural Affairs Commission; we are grateful for their support. Key funding for the publication was provided by the Getty Foundation as a part of its Pacific Standard Time program; we are thankful for its openness in including an architectural writer as an appropriate subject in the granting initiative. Special thanks to Margaret Morgan and Wesley Phoa, and Nicole Katz and Paperchase Press for additional publication support. Thanks to Elizabeth Pulsinelli for astute copyediting, Anthony Carfello and Priscilla Chung for tireless pursuit of copyright permissions, Roman Jaster for precise design, Teira Johnson for assistance with the exhibition layout, and MAK Center staff members Angelica Fuentes and Adam Peña.

Kimberli Meyer and Susan Morgan

Pier at Santa Monica, California, September 5, 1949.
Esther McCoy (foreground) with husband Berkeley Tobey,
Vera Dreiser (left) and Helen Dreiser.

Contents

At the Edge of Her Time
by Kimberli Meyer

The story of a person can be a story of a city; such is the case with Esther McCoy, a prolific writer who was a powerful proponent of modern architecture in Los Angeles. *Sympathetic Seeing* gives us the opportunity not only to take a closer look at an under-recognized contributor to Southern California culture, but also to excavate a history of Los Angeles and present it for renewed viewing. While the Esther McCoy Papers housed at the Archives of American Art contain many topics of interest, this exhibition highlights her activities in and influence on Los Angeles. They include leftist activism and the politics of the built environment; an inside view of the office of architect R.M. Schindler; a tale of two Kings Road houses; and the relationship between writing and architecture and how popular media is used to interpret space.

A modern utopian vision blossomed in the United States during the Great Depression and again after World War II. McCoy, like many of her modernist architect contemporaries, was concerned with the politics of the built environment, insisting that architecture and urban space were not isolated entities but an intrinsic part of the social fabric. Her contributions as a fiction writer, critic, and historian stemmed from her embrace of this worldview. Her interest in leftist politics began early; while still in college, she met writer and avid socialist Theodore Dreiser and became his lifelong friend and sometime research assistant. After her arrival in Los Angeles in 1932, McCoy's activism developed and intensified, and she became involved with the International Labor Defense (ILD), the legal arm of the USA Communist Party. In an unpublished memoir, she describes its office on South Broadway in downtown Los Angeles:

> The glass panel in the heavy oak door to the office has been broken so often in police raids that wood strips are nailed inside. The office is raided about once or twice a month, and the desks and the pine kitchen chairs and swivel desk chairs bear endless raid scars. There is little more in the office than a couple of old typewriters, desks, tables, chairs and a telephone. No files were kept in the office; I think someone even took the letterheads home at night. The Communist Party office on Spring Street was even barer than its legal arm, the ILD.

McCoy details working with Leo Gallagher, a staunch labor rights attorney who worked on IDL cases and ran for the office of superior court judge. Gallagher was well known for defending Tom Mooney, the radical labor leader considered by many to have been wrongly imprisoned for the San Francisco Preparedness Day Bombing of 1916. (Mooney was finally pardoned by the governor of California in 1939.) McCoy wrote various kinds of texts for the IDL, attended community meetings, and helped with Gallagher's campaign. She depicts the "class struggle" not only as difficult, but also as dangerous and violent, with street gatherings broken up by police brutality, and labor movement leaders enduring repeated arrest, beatings, and blacklisting from prominent positions.

Connected to the labor movement were efforts to improve the living conditions of the urban poor, which included advocating for public housing. In the mid-1930s, McCoy spent a year researching the Los Angeles slums, conducting door-to-door surveys, compiling a detailed report, and submitting her findings to the city's housing authority. Many public officials resisted admitting that slums existed, in part because of their commitment to local boosterism and in part because substandard housing in Los Angeles consisted of densely situated, low-rise shacks as opposed to tenement buildings. One city official claimed that only tenements where more than two hundred people were housed under one roof qualified as slums. McCoy published articles and editorials on housing in newspapers and broadsheets, including the leftist publications *United Progressive News* and *Daily News*. She indicated that in 1937 twenty percent of all residences in Los Angeles were unfit for human habitation and advocated for the enactment of the Wagner-Steagall Housing Act, which designated funds for public housing. McCoy's dedication to fair housing led her to apply for a research and writing position with the Research and Statistics Division of the United States Housing Authority in Washington, D.C. Had she been offered and accepted that position, she would have worked under the powerful public housing advocate Catherine Bauer Wurster (and Southern California architecture may have suffered the loss of her attention).

In the 1960s, McCoy was a defender of both the community of Watts and Simon Rodia's landmark Watts Towers. Her ongoing concern with the conditions of the built environment in low-income neighborhoods is documented in archived notes from her conversations with community members. On August 16, 1965—the last day of the Watts Riots—she spoke with Edgar Goff, an African American architect who had worked for Victor Gruen, an Austrian émigré architect known for designing shopping malls across the United States. Goff complained about the lack of urban planning in the Watts area while simultaneously fearing clueless city planners. He described the desperate need for parks and schools, and advised the city to "forget for the moment the sociologists and psychologists, and send in a planner who knows how to interpret the people's way of living." He told McCoy: "I was born in this neighborhood and grew up there. No one has yet listened to what the Negro is saying in his everyday life."

Through McCoy's involvement with politics, she met Pauline Gibling Schindler in the early 1940s. As the wife of R.M. Schindler, Pauline was a client/collaborator in the making of the Schindler House on Kings Road in West Hollywood, California. She was dedicated to art and architecture as well as radical politics and intellectual spirit. She was a member of the Communist party, and quite active in social and political causes. Shortly after McCoy's application to architecture school at the University of Southern California (USC) was "strongly discouraged" due to her gender and age, Pauline informed her of an opening for a draftsperson in Schindler's office. In her descriptions of both the job interview and the job, McCoy draws a picture of the daily life of the Schindler practice. Her stories from the period encapsulate the draftsperson's perspective on her boss, the literary talent's story of an architect, and the budding critic's take on modern architecture. In 1945, while working in Schindler's office, McCoy published her first piece of architectural writing, the essay "Schindler, Space Architect," in *Direction*, a cultural journal with an antifascist editorial position.

Writing a regular column in the *Los Angeles Times*, publishing books, and contributing frequently to professional and mainstream magazines about architecture, McCoy developed a wide audience for California's architectural legacy and its then-new experiments in modern architecture. In discussing contemporary design and its place in the modern home, she spoke directly to female readers about their traditional domain. Architecture must take hold of the public imagination in order to survive, and McCoy's strong and consistent voice enticed a reading public to expand their ideas about architecture and space. This was (and is) particularly important in Los Angeles, where the forces of real estate speculation so often trump architecture.

For McCoy, architectural advocacy sometimes meant taking a preservationist stance. From 1963 to 1970, she was deeply involved with the cause to save the Dodge House on North Kings

Road, just up the street from the Schindler House. Irving Gill built the house for Walter Luther Dodge in 1916. Having written about it in her book *Five California Architects*, McCoy well understood its significance as perhaps the first modern house of the American West. She chronicled its history and importance in her narrative on the house for the Historic American Buildings Survey. The Dodge House was sold to the McKenna Family in 1924 for $125,000. In 1939, the Los Angeles High School District, wanting to acquire the property for a high school, condemned it against the McKennas' will. After the family was paid $69,000, the district reversed its decision about a Kings Road school, and transferred title to the junior college district. For decades, it was used as a domestic training facility for the Los Angeles Trade Technical College, and remained intact. In 1963, when the Board of Education declared the property surplus, efforts to preserve the house went into full force. In the fall of 1963, the Los Angeles County Board of Supervisors approved a zoning change for North Kings Road between Melrose Avenue and Santa Monica Boulevard. The controversial change from R-1 to R-4 greatly increased the property values on the street, and paved the way for the demolition of single-family residences and the construction of condominiums.

The heartbreaking conclusion of the Dodge House story is seen in the photos taken on Monday, February 9, 1970, when, in the quiet of a rainy morning, the magnificent structure was bulldozed. Nobody saw it coming that particular morning, so it was a relatively quick death, with few witnesses. A *Los Angeles Times* story tells of architecture students from USC making a scheduled visit on Wednesday, February 11, to the Dodge House only to find it gone, transforming a "tour into a wake." In McCoy's papers, the conversations about the Dodge House from 1963 to 1970 have been collected and carefully preserved. These files include wide-ranging correspondence with cultural leaders across the continent and appeals to finance a documentary film that would raise awareness and rally support for the Dodge

Schindler House (R.M. Schindler, 1922),
West Hollywood, California.

House. For *Sympathetic Seeing*, a selection of these documents appears in the exhibition and as a booklet within this catalog. They offer a series of vignettes of the process of defining and defending architecture that reveal the complexities of assigning value to architecture's existence relative to greater urban forces.

In the great condominium-ization of North Kings Road, there is a reason why the existential crisis of the Dodge House did not extend to the Schindler House: Pauline Schindler. Even after she was divorced from R.M., Pauline continued to be a strong admirer of his work. Her vision of the Schindler House extended from the conception of a cooperative, two-family dwelling built to accommodate dialogue across difference, through decades of hosting and housing artistic intellectuals and their activities, to the physical and discursive preservation of the house. Pauline had the foresight to anticipate the transformations of the city and saw to it that the Schindler House would be protected after her death. A radical homemaker, Pauline was part of a phenomenon of women coming out of the Left who were staking a claim in architecture. Her cohorts included patrons Aline Barnsdall and the Press sisters Leah Lovell and Harriet Freeman.

Between the three of them, they commissioned a passel of significant works by Frank Lloyd Wright, R.M. Schindler, and Richard Neutra in the first few decades of the twentieth century.

When Esther McCoy stepped off the train in Los Angeles in 1932, she entered a city bursting with innovative architectural ideas and engaged in an energetic battle for the rights of the poor and working classes. McCoy embraced this spirit and her willingness to fight for a more democratic system ultimately helped make a difference. In 1935, the Wagner Act, or National Labor Relations Act, gave workers the right to organize for collective bargaining. In 1937, the Wagner-Steagall Housing Act became law, opening the door for subsidized public housing. (The name of Representative Henry B. Steagall, R-AL, is often in the news these days because of the Glass-Steagall Act of 1933, which regulated banks and would have prevented the 2008 economic collapse had it not been repealed under the Clinton administration in 1999.) McCoy's work may remind the contemporary reader that enormous risks have been taken, basic freedoms have been hard won, and although much ground has been gained, much of that is under threat.

Sympathetic Seeing is a kind of local excavation where past and present mingle. The MAK Center's practice is rooted in its relationship with the Schindler House, and in this show the house is one of the primary objects in the exhibition. It was the workplace of several of our exhibition's cast of characters. It was influenced and aided by the Dodge House, which is now lost to us despite McCoy's efforts. And it embodies the best of the modernist project: influential experimentation in architecture and a program for social justice in space. This exhibition is a coming-together of old comrades, starring a woman at the edge of her time who challenged many to open their minds and think forward.

The Visible Scene
by Susan Morgan

The door was ajar. I entered.[1]
—Esther McCoy

In the spring of 1944, Esther McCoy first walked into R.M. Schindler's
Kings Road studio, seeking a job as a draftsperson and fully braced
for rejection. She had learned of the vacancy through Pauline Gibling
Schindler, the architect's estranged wife, adjacent neighbor, and indom-
itable champion. Years later, McCoy recalled the scene: "The euge-
nia hedge at the north side of 833–835 was neatly clipped to head height
with not a sprig out of place, while the one to the south grew wild and
tall with tufts shooting out everywhere. Two people of different tastes
and of equal strength obviously controlled the landscaping of the house
on Kings Road." In McCoy's writing, each hard-working word delivers;
nothing is wasted or left to chance. Her lean depictions are as particular
and evocative as fairy tales. "It was as if the house stood up by the pres-
sure of opposing wills,"[2] she observed, precisely framing the auspicious
day. Schindler, of course, hired her on the spot.

      McCoy had been writing and publishing for more than
twenty years when she went to work in Schindler's office. At nineteen,
she'd boldly written to Theodore Dreiser: an admiring note from a college student on summer break in Fayetteville, Arkansas, to a famous
"radically American" writer and political progressive. The fifty-three-
year-old Dreiser—living in New York, entangled in various love affairs,

and facing the deadline for *An American Tragedy*—replied promptly
with his signature idiosyncratic spelling:

> Your a quaint & elusive maybe just a slightly affected person.
> I can't say. But I like your letters. And I think I can tell you
> what you are going to be—eventually if not now—or right
> soon. A writer. Your mental compass seems to point thusly.
> You have such a flare for the visible scene & present it with
> so much simplicity & force. You might as well begin scrib-
> bling forthwith. Only, of course, one does need variety of
> contact & experience. By no other method are worthwhile
> tales to be come by. You know that, too. I know you do. [3]

McCoy deftly sidestepped Dreiser's flirtations (as one
Dreiser biographer noted, the author considered fan mail an "aphrodi-
siac" but "Miss McCoy remained aloof" [4]) and they maintained a lively,
professional correspondence and a longtime friendship. In 1926, when
McCoy left the University of Michigan and moved to Greenwich
Village, she occasionally worked as Dreiser's research assistant, odd-
jobbed for book publishers, copy edited pulp magazines, and composed
unsigned reviews and unsold fiction. She saved up her earnings and
traveled to Paris and Key West; she wrote short stories while sitting at
Les Deux Magots and a first novel in the seclusion of a Floridian conch
house. In 1932, she went out to Los Angeles, intending to spend just
one winter, and stayed for the rest of her life.

In California, McCoy continued to observe and
strongly present the visible scene. Her writing appeared in progressive journals and literary quarterlies; her voice was always direct and
each reported situation palpably inhabited. At the height of the Great
Depression, McCoy embarked on the itinerant life of a freelance writer,
acquiring assignments, part-time work, and temporary homes. She
spent the winters of 1932 and 1933 in a dune shack on an empty stretch
of beach ten miles north of Malibu. While still settling in, she sent

a long letter to her friend Josephine Herbst, a New York writer rusticating in Erwinna, Pennsylvania:

> I've been alone at a cottage on the beach for a week. It's a desolate swell looking place for a pauper. I got it through some crazy fluke, and may stay here most of the winter though I am always ready to move from any place at a moment's notice. It seems a bit unjust that the fine frigidaire should be practically barren inside and that the handsome electric stove should have mostly beans cooked on it and that all the other electric gadgets should be of no use to me.
>
> The best thing of all is a stereopticon whatnot with several hundred pictures of the United States. A picture of Coney Island in 1910 moves me profoundly. Also a book of arithmetic problems belonging to a son of the owner. I have reached the long division section. I don't like the fractions so much because I can't win at them. The radio fascinates me but I can't get over the feeling that I'm opening someone else's mail when I twist the dial....[5]

The immediacy and consideration of McCoy's writing allows a reader to look over her shoulder and revisit where she's been. Her senses are keen and the words seem to enter into a space, walk the floor, linger over objects, and reflect the changing light. She was also quick to master the practical novelist's knack for utilizing everyday experience, keeping a collection of aperçus on hand for future use and knowing how to refashion insults into barbed humor. A 1932 diary entry about how she first fell in love with California materializes beautifully in "Honor Is an Echo," a 1945 short story for *Harper's Bazaar*. When a woman on a western-bound cross-country train journey steps out onto the railway platform, McCoy writes: "I walked up and down the station platform at San Bernardino in the light night air, and the smell of the orange blossoms left me too buoyant to sleep." In 1951, her ongoing exasperation with mortgage officers and banks was eventually published as a satirical public service essay titled "How Not to Get a Loan."

McCoy remarked that she had a natural interest in how things were put together, sorting out exactly how a story or a house was constructed. Her father had been in the lumber business, owning sawmills and lumberyards, and she had grown up in a wide brick six-bedroom house, built in 1901, with a hipped roof and three small gables, in Coffeyville, Kansas. Her father's wood-paneled office featured his bulky standard typewriter kept within a roll-top desk beneath a picture of Will Rogers; her mother's portable typewriter sat out on a low sewing table overseen by a portrait of President Woodrow Wilson. "One thing we missed," she observed in the 1970s while describing her childhood home to a friend, the urban designer Diana Balmori: "No unexpected cubby holes except in a turn in the closet under the stairs and on the third floor a deep cupboard over the northwest bedroom (my brothers). All else was open and rational; probably why I had an affinity for the international style."[6]

When McCoy was newly arrived in California, she liked the look of the Monterey-style houses in Santa Monica with their austere Yankee facades constructed out of lime-washed adobe and wrapped with second-story wooden balconies borrowed from the Caribbean. As she continued to look around the city, she encountered new architecture still under construction. "I had the good fortune in the early thirties to find Neutra on my own; I was an instant believer," she later wrote in *Vienna to Los Angeles: Two Journeys*, her 1979 book about the early relationship between Schindler and Richard Neutra. "I had come upon a newly finished but unoccupied apartment house on which, as I recall, the occupancy permit had been held up. A door was open and I entered; I entered twice. Undisturbed, I would take up one position and stand a long time and look, then I would move to another. The band of windows in his typical module was so acerbic to the eye that I could stand for minutes tasting the new sharpness.

There was a moral participation of the senses—the puritan ethic was aesthetic. Beauty was morality during the Depression years."

During the late 1930s, McCoy had learned architectural drafting from a boyfriend, a romantic intellectual contractor who was building cabins at Mozumdar Lodge, a mountain retreat for an Indian-born spiritual leader and his followers. After their romance ended, she purchased a turn-of-the-century bungalow in the Ocean Park section of Santa Monica. The price was $1500. She paid with her own savings and set to work designing the renovation herself. "The plans could easily have been squeezed into three pages, but with all my cross-sections and details, I stretched them out to six," she wrote. "I did this mainly because I wanted to keep the drawing close to me, hoping that the pencil under my hand would teach me something more than how to set down the condition, when a wall meets a floor or a roof. I was hoping that if I'd listen carefully, I would get a clue to why one building was wonderful and another ordinary. That is, the pencil yielded no secrets."[7]

In 1941, McCoy married Berkeley Greene Tobey. Born into an old New England family and active in New York's early avant-garde literary and radical political circles, Tobey was twenty-three years her senior. McCoy was the primary wage earner for their household and, in 1942, she found wartime employment as an engineering draftsman at Douglas Aircraft, detailing wings on the C-74 cargo ship. Wartime demands had suddenly generated new technologies, speeded up production schedules, and revolutionized design. "What was out of date was ruthlessly discarded," wrote McCoy. "In the rush to modernize all branches of industry, prewar products were dumped, old dies melted down. A new page had turned. And the arts, the handcrafts, machine crafts, the sciences and literature had turned too. Like half a dozen children napping on the same pallet, the movement of one roused the rest. They did not move in unison but all stirred awake. The sounds that had waked them were the bombs at Pearl Harbor."[8]

When McCoy began to write about architecture in 1945, she found a responsive subject waiting for her. She was a primary witness to mid-century design ("the marriage between Walden Pond and Douglas Aircraft"[9]) as it was being created, and her attentive writing followed closely, entering the rooms and capturing both appearances and experience. "At the beginning of the war I did a remodel of a fifty year old house for my husband and me," she explained in a 1948 dossier prepared for a mainstream magazine. "Incidentally, he complains that whenever we go out I am consulted on what will happen if a bearing wall is pulled down, how much it will cost to move the laundry to the kitchen, or what space will be gained by changing the walk-in closet to a wardrobe. I owe my clarity in writing on architecture to my husband, who sets his intelligence in that field at the age of seven. Anything he doesn't understand, I edit out."[10]

For over forty years, McCoy published countless articles, essays, and reviews and served as a contributing editor and correspondent for the leading design magazines: *Arts & Architecture, Zodiac, Lotus, Progressive Architecture,* and *Architectural Forum.* During the 1950s, she wrote about California's neglected architectural heritage and chronicled *Arts & Architecture*'s legendary Case Study House program.

McCoy once said that she wanted her writing to be as smooth as glass on top while everything boiled beneath the surface. Her work anticipated what Truman Capote later proposed as the nonfiction novel. "Journalism always moves along a horizontal plane telling a story," said Capote. "While fiction—good fiction—moves vertically, taking you deeper and deeper into character and events."[11] McCoy had long discerned that intersection between fiction and nonfiction; she prized the facts and recognized the heart of the story where the visible scene suddenly comes to life. When her classic *Five California Architects* was first published in 1960, Pauline Gibling Schindler, who was among the many readers to send an admiring note, wrote: "The objectivity and scrupulousness of the writing, combined with the restrained tenderness and the awareness in depth, give the book a particular richness. I believe that each of the five, and perhaps especially the last of them, would have been happy with what you have communicated of their work, their purposes, and the underlying feeling." [12] McCoy's prose shimmers with a graceful intelligence and her considerable gift for listening and looking closely. Writing from the inside, she delivered a rare, compelling, and fully inhabited history.

1 Esther McCoy, "Schindler: A Personal Reminiscence," *L.A. Architect*, November 1987, 5–9.

2 Esther McCoy, "Happy Birthday RMS," unpublished memoir, n.d., Esther McCoy Papers, Archives of American Art, Smithsonian Institution, Washington D.C.

3 Theodore Dreiser in *Theodore Dreiser: Letters to Women, New Letters*, ed. Thomas Riggio (Urbana and Chicago: University of Illinois Press, 2008), 181.

4 W.A. Swanberg, *Dreiser* (New York: Scribner, 1965), 285.

5 Esther McCoy letter to Josephine Herbst, c. 1933, McCoy Papers.

6 Esther McCoy letter to Diana Balmori, n.d, McCoy Papers.

7 McCoy, "Happy Birthday RMS."

8 Esther McCoy, "The Rationalist Period," in *High Styles: 20th Century American Design*, ed. Lisa Phillips and David A. Hanks (New York: Whitney Museum of American Art, 1985), exhibition catalog, 130.

9 Esther McCoy, "West Coast Architects V: John Lautner," *Arts & Architecture*, August 1965.

10 Esther McCoy, "a little dossier," unfinished letter, c. 1948, McCoy Papers.

11 Gloria Steinem, "A Visit with Truman Capote," *Glamour*, April 1966.

12 Pauline Gibling Schindler letter to Esther McCoy, August 1, 1960, McCoy Papers.

PART 1

Southern California, a Curious Period

Dorothy Poynton, Los Angeles Summer Olympics, 1932. The seventeen-year-old "diving marvel" from Pasadena, California, wins the gold medal.

Amelia Earhart, Long Beach, California, 1932. August 1932: Amelia Earhart sets the record for the fastest woman's nonstop transcontinental flight, flying from Los Angeles, California, to Newark, New Jersey, in 19 hours and 5 minutes. A year later, Earhart bested her own transcontinental record by flying across the country in 17 hours and 7½ minutes.

Earthquake in Long Beach, California, 1933. Photo by Esther McCoy. By 1933, the population of Los Angeles exceeded 1 million and the sprawling city was confirmed a genuine metropolitan center. The 6.3 magnitude Long Beach earthquake destroyed heavily populated areas and caused over 100 fatalities.

Upton Sinclair campaign billboards, Olive Hill, Hollywood, California, 1934. Socialist writer Upton Sinclair (1878–1968) was the Democratic candidate for California governor in 1934. Among his outspoken, high-profile supporters was Aline Barnsdall, a freethinking oil heiress. Barnsdall used Olive Hill, her thirty-six-acre Hollywood property, as a staging ground for billboards displaying the political and cultural positions she actively supported.

	1904	Esther McCoy born November 18, in Horatio, Arkansas. Raised in Coffeyville, Kansas.
	1917–25	McCoy educated in the Midwest: attends boarding school in Lexington, Missouri, and University of Michigan, Ann Arbor.
	1926	McCoy moves to New York; enters into the avant-garde Bohemian life of Greenwich Village; and works as a bookstore clerk, copy editor, and for Theodore Dreiser as a researcher.
	1928–30	McCoy spends extended periods in Paris and Key West, Florida, writing fiction.
1932		Los Angeles population reaches 1.2 million. The city's rapid growth is described as "the greatest internal migration in United States history."
	1932	After being hospitalized with double pneumonia in New York, McCoy travels to Los Angeles to recuperate.
1932		X Summer Olympics held in Los Angeles.
1932		Amelia Earhart flies from Los Angeles to Newark, the first woman to complete a solo nonstop transcontinental flight.
1933		Long Beach Earthquake strikes.
1934		Socialist writer Upton Sinclair runs unsuccessfully for California Governor.
	1934	McCoy continues to work intermittently for Dreiser as a freelance researcher and reader. Writes for progressive newspapers and magazines.
	1938	McCoy moves to the Ocean Park section of Santa Monica, California.
1938		House Committee on Un-American Activities founded to begin anti-Communist investigations.

What excited me about Santa Monica was the way the mountains tipped down into the ocean. The Needham shop was half a block from Palisades Park, a narrow landscaped strip high above the beach. I could stand in the park and face the sea and an adorable saddle in the low mountains. I hugged it to my heart.

—Esther McCoy, "About Malibu," unpublished memoir, Esther McCoy Papers,
    Archives of American Art, Smithsonian Institution.

Santa Monica, California, coastline, May 1933.
Southern California's Theodore Roosevelt Highway
was opened in 1929. A scenic coastal road
extending from Santa Monica Canyon to Oxnard,
it provided public access to the Rancho Malibu
land owned by May Rindge. In 1935, the Roosevelt
Highway became California State Route 1.

ccc DAILY NEWS, LOS ANGELES, CALIF. MONDAY, AUGUST 16, 1937

COURT OF PUBLIC OPINION

SHOULD RENTS COME DOWN?

Yes

By ESTHER M'COY
Executive Board Member, Federation Against the High Cost of Living.

The Federation Against the High Cost of Living recently made a survey of rent raises in Los Angeles residences. It showed that rents have increased, on an average, between 32 and 35 per cent in the last year. One group of 24 homes in the survey showed that the 24 tenants paid $399 a month for their houses and apartments a year ago. Today they are paying a total of $620 a month.

Why are rents high? One of the chief reasons is that there is a housing shortage in the United States and in Los Angeles. Between 1923 and 1929, some 450,000 families were accommodated with new dwellings each year. But in the next seven years only 75,000 families gained new dwellings each year. A housing shortage was in the making.

"The inevitable consequence of a housing shortage," says President William Green of the American Federation of Labor, "is a drastic increase in rents. In the absence of an adequate remedy, rents are bound to go up faster than wages."

The remedy is more houses. The federation stands for lower rents, for opposition to evictions due to unwarrantable rent rises, for the enforcement of the health and fire laws. But it also advocates the enactment of the Wagner-Steagall housing bill. It advocates houses for those tens of thousands of persons

ESTHER M'COY

who live in our five slum areas, for people who live on an income of less than $1000 a year and are unable to find adequate housing.

There are 550,000 housing units in Los Angeles. The steady population is 1,500,000. The floating population is from 100,000 to 200,000.

Look at the human side of these figures.

Seven people until recently lived in a dwelling of approximately 1500 cubic feet on Pecan Street. Five hundred cubic feet is the minimum cubic feet a person, required by law. There is no bathtub. The toilet is outside. The company renting it says "No relief clients." Why? Because an investigator wouldn't "pass it." Yet they advanced the rent 100 per cent.

In Venice a family of four living on $25 a week are forced in with another family to get a house within their income. The rent is $50 a month. There are six rooms. Seven people live there. Their rent problem has been further complicated by the child ban among Los Angeles landlords. Last November the Literary Digest said that only 48 of the 4800 apartment houses in Los Angeles would permit children.

In a four-room house on South Gless street the plumbing is out of order. Rain leaks through the broken plaster in every room in the house. Last year the house rented for $10. The tenant was informed that without repairs it would now rent for $15. With repairs—all of which are required by law—the rent would be $25. A family of nine lives there. Their income is $60 a month. They are moving. The rent in the new house is $25 a month. They had difficulty finding that house. The remaining $35, after the rent is paid, must feed, clothe and meet all other expenses of nine people.

There are 25,000 buildings in our five slum areas. State and city housing and health laws, fire laws are broken with impunity by the landlords. The housing shortage is throwing more and more people into these blighted areas.

The answer? The answer is always the same—increased tuberculosis, communicable diseases, crime. . . .

What of the cost in day-to-day human misery? What is the happiness of tens of thousands of people in the city worth?

"Hands off housing" is what the real estate interests say. In the March Apartment Journal a writer says: "The threat of governmental housing projects will hang more heavily over the heads of the local apartment owners. I would like to state here definitely that I am opposed to any invasion of the Government in the field of housing . . ."

And in speaking of the housing legislation recently passed almost unanimously by both California Legislatures and pocket-vetoed by Gov. Frank F. Merriam, the August Building Contractors Forum says: "The building contractors of California can now sigh with relief and attend to their building business with a free mind, for once again any peril of crackpot legislation is removed."

Realizing the seriousness of the housing shortage, the rent menace, the prevailing unsanitary conditions in our city, a Los Angeles municipal housing commissioner suggested that a committee of several members of the Housing Commission and the Federation Against the High Cost of Living be set up to work together for adequate housing.

Progressive legislators and public officials and prominent churchmen have interested themselves in the Federation Against the High Cost of Living. With us, they say, rents must come down!

No

By J. W. PIERCE
President Apartment Association of Los Angeles County

Rents admittedly have gone up, but they are by no means too high. Nor have they increased as much as many tenants seem to believe. The average furnished apartment in Los Angeles rents for around $30 or $35 a month. An apartment that rents for $30 now cost $26 or $27 a year ago.

A survey we made in Glendale a short time ago showed that apartment house rents have risen 23 per cent from the low they hit during the depression. Glendale rents, we find, are typical of the Los Angeles metropolitan area. Possibly there has been a 1 or 2 per cent increase since the survey was taken.

But take a glance at the increases in the other items in the cost of living. To begin with, the United States Bureau of Labor Statistics reports that rents in Los Angeles slumped off, at the depths of the depression, by 55.8 per cent of what they were in the normal years of 1923-1925. No other item in the cost of living fell so far. The cost of living as a whole decreased but 30.2 per cent. Food fell 39 per cent, clothing 31 per cent, fuel and light 28 per cent, furnishings 39 per cent.

Since those dark days every item in the cost of living has increased, but rents have lagged behind all others. The Government figures for Los Angeles show rents to be but slightly more than half of what they were in the 1923-1925 days, while prices of food and clothing are better than 80 per cent of their old normal figure.

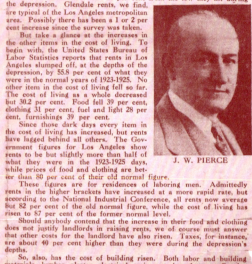

J. W. PIERCE

These figures are for residences of laboring men. Admittedly rents in the higher brackets have increased at a more rapid rate, but according to the National Industrial Conference, all rents now average but 82 per cent of the old normal figure, while the cost of living has risen to 87 per cent of the former normal level.

Should anybody contend that the increase in their food and clothing does not justify landlords in raising rents, we of course must answer that other costs for the landlord have also risen. Taxes, for instance, are about 40 per cent higher than they were during the depression's depths.

So, also, has the cost of building risen. Both labor and building materials—lumber, plaster, electrical equipment—has shot up. So also have the prices of furnishings for apartments. Roughly, building costs are 95 per cent of what they were during the normal pre-depression years.

Moreover, the depression years left many apartments in a bad state of repair. Landlords often lost many of their properties, or, if they hung on to them, were unable to keep them in shape. Consequently they are forced now to pay for painting, repairs, new furniture, etc., which normally they would have been able to finance as they went along.

But it is the law of supply and demand that gives the chief denial to the charges that rents are too high. There was a time when there was a vacancy percentage in Los Angeles of 30 per cent. That day has past. Apartment houses are nearly full. Naturally, rents rise, because tenants are willing to pay more. A landlord may offer an apartment to a prospective tenant for $25 and receive an offer of $27.50 and again of $30 while the first comer is "thinking it over."

This is particularly true on the East Side, where the arrival of new industries has attracted workers to the district. It is also true in the Wilshire and West Hollywood district, where people who have obtained better jobs and are making more money are flocking.

It should be borne in mind that both industrial wages and payrolls, as shown by Government figures, are higher now than in the normal years of 1923-25.

Those who say rents should come down overlook the fact that real estate values are based on the income that property can return. Lower rents would depreciate the value of all residential property, which in turn would have a depressing effect on conditions and soon strike wage earners, particularly the low-salaried earners, who are always the first to be affected in a business slump. Lower rents would mean more general distress.

There are two chief arguments against public housing as a means of lowering rent. First is that public housing requires Government subsidies, which are paid by all the people. The burden is merely shifted and scattered. Second, public housing, even with subsidies, in the past has never been able to achieve its purpose of providing low-cost housing. In New York, the Knickerbocker public housing project was intended to be rented for $6.50 a room; when it was built it was necessary to charge $12 a room. Thus the people who benefited were those who could afford to pay equal rents to private landlords; the original slum tenants merely had to find other slums.

I think that shows that the problem of high rents is really one of lack of income. Wages must be higher, not rents lower.

I think it is worth noting that it is generally agreed that home ownership is desirable. And home ownership always increases when rent go up. Tenants, refusing to pay the rent to a landlord, build their own homes. But bringing rents down would decrease the desire for home ownership. I do not think we want that.

« Esther McCoy, "Court of Public Opinion—Should Rents Come Down?," editorial, *Los Angeles Daily News*, August 16, 1937. *Los Angeles Daily News*, an independent tabloid, was originally founded in 1923 by Cornelius Vanderbilt IV as the *Los Angeles Illustrated Daily News*; it ceased publication in 1954. In 1926, when editor E. Manchester Boddy took over, the *Los Angeles Daily News* gained a lively reputation for its pro-New Deal outlook and impudent headlines.

Esther McCoy and Marshall Ho'o, Zuma Beach, Malibu, California, c. 1933. During the 1930s, Ho'o (1910–93) was head of the Federation of Chinese Youth Clubs and a labor activist; he worked in a Santa Monica butcher shop where Asian American employees were required to pay AFL-CIO dues but were denied union benefits. Ho'o later became a Tai Chi Chuan master, doctor of Chinese medicine, and author. He taught Tai Chi for over forty years and is widely recognized as the "dean of Tai Chi teachers."

Esther McCoy, Santa Monica, California, 1938.
In 1938, McCoy and Allan Read published *The Golden Goose Murders*, "An Inspector Franklin Brady Mystery." The two women, writing together under the pseudonym "Allan McRoyd," published two more books in the Greystone Press series: *The Double Shadow Murders* (1939) and *Death in Costume* (1940).

From the oral history with Esther McCoy conducted by Joseph Giovannini:

Esther McCoy: The Depression was a curious period, where everyone had lots of time, and there was nothing much to do. And in California, where there was no editorial work to do, it was almost impossible to earn a living in the way that I would have in New York. No publishing. So I did odd jobs writing and editing manuscripts for people who wanted to write. Then I began, through the Needhams, to get into the radical movement.

You have only to see someone beaten up, a speaker beaten up, pulled from the platform and beaten up, to incense you, and turn you to the left. But it was a period where everyone was more or less a protestor. In Malibu, people would stop off who had no money whatever; they were hitchhiking from one place to another to look for work. It was a terribly sad period, but there was a great deal of camaraderie too, during that time.

When I went to New York, I had...sympathies with Sacco and Vanzetti. One reason I chose the *New York World* when I got to New York was because of their coverage of Sacco and Vanzetti. When I was working at Brentano's, I would get the paper every morning and look for things on Sacco and Vanzetti. And then I went to Union Square, finally, the night when they were executed. I was working then on a magazine, and it was near there, and I'd gone with a colleague from the magazine to Union Square. I remember how incensed I was because the cops said to this girl, "What are you, a good Irish girl, doing here?" and she laughed at him. I was shocked at her fraternizing. [Laughs]

Joseph Giovannini: So there was a rally, then, at Union Square?

EM: No, a vigil at Union Square. I'd gone home after work, but then I went back that evening. I think there were...cannons on all the buildings around Union Square, on the tops of buildings, pointed down, you know, for a possible riot.

JG: So before the Depression, you had a strong political instinct?

EM: Yes. Let's see, what else can I tell you about that.

JG: Were your political leanings similar to those of your parents?

EM: No, it was farther left, and then during the Depression, it became much more left. From the Needhams. There were all the political groups that came into their bookshop.... There was no one who wasn't on the Left, even Entenza, who was not really political. The thirties was a period of protestors.

JG: Was Southern California a sort of conservative place at that time?

EM: Yes, it was—the *Los Angeles Times* called it "the last white hope," you know; it was a non-union town.

—Oral history interview with Esther McCoy, June 7 – November 14, 1987, Esther McCoy Papers, Archives of American Art, Smithsonian Institution.

Slums Are Cancer Spots

By ESTHER McCOY

HALF A DOZEN people in Los Angeles are sufficiently aware of our housing needs to make any effort to clean up the slums.

HOUSING is not political. If housing were dependent on the words of politicians, Los Angeles would not now have what one English housing expert calls slums potentially as bad as any in Europe.

There are perhaps as many people on the Municipal Housing Commission to block slum clearance as there are ones to further it.

THE MAYOR has spoken. Recently he sent a letter to the Housing Commission asking them to work out a low-cost housing project. He has protected himself.

Yet he has done nothing toward removing our tens of thousands of slum dwellers from hovels, shacks and deserted building—where they are bedded down like rats—and

say flat-footedly that a slum is a "residential area where the houses and conditions of life are of a squalid and wretched character, which hence has become a social liability to the community."

LOOK at the two liabilities pictured on this page. Both are slums. Both have a front and back yard. Neither house 200 people.

The one with the cactus in the yard is typical of houses in the Ficket Street slum area, a small area but one of the worst in the city. Twelve people live in this four-room house.

The other, with the lean-to outhouse, is on Imperial Highway east of Central Avenue. Here a man and his wife and five children live in two rooms.

THERE are more slums in Los Angeles than there

SEVEN PEOPLE live in this two-room shack on Imperial Highway east of Central.

providing them with modern sanitary dwellings.

"Los Angeles has no true slum district," the Mayor's representative, Harold H. Story, tells me.

A slum is not a slum if it has a front yard and a back yard, he says. Furthermore, it takes 200 people under the same roof to make a slum.

THE CITY COUNCIL admits no slums in the city. They are convinced that only when people are piled vertically in buildings that reach to the sky, story upon story, do you have a slum. Level the filth and decay down to one-story shacks, spread it over acres, and you have at the most sub-standard buildings.

Some time in the future, when we get around to it, they can be cleaned up. The Duke of Windsor

are people who like the sound of the word.

"Public officials are persuaded that it is unwise to refer to the existence of slums," editors of Fortune magazine say. The facts do not always harmonize with the melody to which the local boosters sing their lays. And the result has been that municipal authorities have all too frequently proceeded upon the theory that what they don't know won't hurt them.

Let's look at the factual sour notes.

A half million dwellings in the city of Los Angeles are unsanitary and disease-breeding. For the interests of adequate housing and health alone this number of dwellings is needed, according to a local official.

This figure leaves out of account the many thousands of sub-standard dwellings which are by anyone's definition of the word "blight-

PART OF the worst slum district in the city. 12 people live in this four-room house on Ficket Street.

is coming in November to take a look at our housing, so let's forget the cancer spots and think about Bel-Air.

Professional housers of the nation aren't so choosy about their definitions. To members of ex-President Hoover's Conference on Home Building, the space around a house for cactus and geranium didn't alleviate conditions inside. They

ed." You can see this genteel squalor any day you want to walk down West First or around Bunker Hill.

The county, including the city, could get along with a bare minimum of a million houses, a special agent of the county says.

UNDER the Wagner-Steagall Housing Act, Los Angeles

may some day get a small fraction of the dwellings absolutely necessary for sanitary conditions. If the whole allotment of the monies to be lent under the Act were turned over to Los Angeles, we would still fall short of our requirements.

As for the County, it is without hope. Governor Merriam is responsible. Last summer he pocket vetoed enabling housing legislation passed almost unanimously by both houses of the California legislature.

These bills, which called for no appropriations, would have given all California a chance to participate in the Wagner-Steagall low-cost housing and slum-clearance program. Los Angeles, because of its local Housing Commission, is the only city or area in the state which can accept aid from the government for housing.

The real estate and building interests—who have never made any attempt to furnish housing for those most direly in need of it—bleated about government invasion. The Apartment Journal speaks of the "threat of governmental housing." The Building Contractors Forum salutes the Governor's pocket veto with " . . . once again any peril of crackpot legislation is removed."

Violated on every hand as they are, the city at least has building and health ordinances. As for the country, 30% of all dwellings have

no inside toilets. 50% have no bath tubs. 20% of all dwellings are unfit for human habitation.

In one instance 18 people occupy a two-room shack 12 by 18 feet, situated on a 40 by 100 foot lot which has four other such houses on it.

FOUR DECADES ago Hamburg's slums repaid the city's neglect in the form of an epidemic of cholera, which cost it millions in shipping.

Today Supervisor John Anson Ford says that the area in his district of greatest congestion (east of Record Street) has the greatest number of tuberculosis cases. In another small area, in the county where 250 families live, there is an average load of 115 active tuberculosis patients.

There the houses are mostly of flimsy construction and many are not waterproof. Mr. Ford says they are commonly infested with pests and bugs harboring in filth in the walls. Floors are frequently in poor repair. The average family has 5.2 persons while 78% of the houses consist of four rooms or less. There are usually two or more houses on a lot. Because of low incomes there is often more than one family in one of these small houses.

This district of recent years has shown consistently the highest percentage of tuberculosis, syphilis

and gonorrhea of any district in the county health area.

On April first there were 118 active cases of tuberculosis under Chest Clinic supervision. 734 negative cases were under supervision. The total Chest Clinic load was 1,048.

HOUSING is as inescapably a problem of health as pure water. To abolish disease-breeding slums is a benefit to all of the people in the city and county.

Will Los Angeles wait for dreaded epidemics before the public conscience is aroused? Our sunshine has not closed the Chest Clinics. The geranium in the front yard and back yard is no protection against tuberculosis, syphilis, infantile paralysis, spinal meningitis, scarlet fever . . .

It took decades to get free clinics. Clinics are but one branch of a tree whose root is unsanitary housing.

Officials doze. The public is sound asleep. Money for hospitals, playgrounds, parks. But for housing . . . little or none. And the cancer spot eats its way into the city.

(This is the first of two articles on housing. The second will appear next week.)

Esther McCoy, "Slums Are Cancer Spots," editorial, *United Progressive News*, October 25, 1937. Published weekly from 1935 to 1938, under the editorship of Reuben W. Borough, *United Progressive News* was the official publication for the United Organizations for Political Action.

PART 2

As the War Was Winding Down

Douglas Aircraft Company started development on a new massive transport plane, the C-74 Globemaster, in 1942. During World War II, McCoy worked at Douglas as an engineering draftsman assigned to the C-74's wing design.

The United States Congress passed the Alien Registration Act after the German Army had occupied Paris in 1940. A federal sedition law, it prohibited any speech or publication that threatened to overthrow the government and ordered all resident aliens to be fingerprinted and registered annually.

Notice for Alien Enemy Registration, Los Angeles, 1942. All Japanese, German, and Italian nationals fourteen years old or older were required to register.

1939	McCoy rents a 1908 bungalow in the Ocean Park section of Santa Monica, California.
1941	With money saved from her employment with Dreiser, McCoy is able to purchase the house for $1500.

1941   December 7, Japan bombs Pearl Harbor.

1941	McCoy marries Berkeley Greene Tobey, a New Englander twenty-three years her senior. Described by McCoy as "a former editor and bon vivant," Tobey had been briefly married to Dorothy Day, founder of the Catholic Worker Movement. In New York, he had worked variously as managing editor for *The Masses* and as a social work administrator. McCoy and Tobey remain together until his death in 1962.

1941   February, U.S. Executive Order 9006 is enforced. The presidential decree calls for the evacuation and internment of all Japanese nationals and Japanese American citizens currently residing on the West Coast.

1942–44	McCoy is employed as engineering draftsperson in the Experimental Shop at Douglas Aircraft.
1944	McCoy applies to study at the University of Southern California School of Architecture. As a forty-year-old woman, she finds that her application is "strongly discouraged."
1944–47	R.M. Schindler employs McCoy as a draftsperson in his Kings Road office. Among the projects she works on while there: Bethlehem Baptist Church (1944–45), Kallis House (1948–51), Laurelwood Apartments (1945–49), Toole House (1946–49); and the Pressburger House (1945–47).
1945	McCoy's career as an architectural writer begins when her article "Schindler, Space Architect" appears in *Direction*, an East Coast-based journal dedicated to "the arts and letters of the left."

1947   House Committee on Un-American Activities begins to subpoena film industry professionals and hold hearings about their alleged involvement with the Communist Party. The major studios declare that they will not "knowingly employ a Communist" and proceed to blacklist scores of actors, screenwriters, and directors.

Living room, McCoy Residence, 2434 Beverly
Avenue, Santa Monica, California. McCoy bought
the house, a two-bedroom bungalow sited on a
rise with a view of the ocean, in 1941, and lived
there for the rest of her life.

McCoy Residence, Santa Monica, California. McCoy's husband,
Berkeley Greene Tobey, "a literary person, great chess player,
radical, and bon vivant," at home, seated on the backyard wall.
"At the beginning of the war I did a remodel of a fifty year old house
for my husband and me," wrote McCoy. R.M. Schindler designed
a later renovation.

Landfair Apartments (Richard J. Neutra, 1937),
Westwood, California. Neutra's International Style
design elegantly utilized alternating bands of glass
and stucco.

I had the good fortune in the early thirties to find Neutra on my own; I was an instant believer. I had come upon a newly finished but unoccupied apartment house on which, as I recall, the occupancy permit had been held up. A door was open and I entered; I entered twice. Undisturbed, I would take up one position and stand a long time and look, then I would move to another. The band of windows in his typical module was so acerbic to the eye that I could stand for minutes tasting the new sharpness. There was a moral participation of the senses—the puritan ethic was aesthetic. Beauty was morality during the Depression years.

—From Esther McCoy, *Vienna to Los Angeles: Two Journeys*, Arts & Architecture Press, Santa Monica, California, 1979, p. 72.

Schindler's complexities took more understanding in the thirties.

His deep roads into space led away from the quickly grasped monoplanar certainties. He was out of context with the resolve of the Depression, a time in which the machine and machined objects were a moral imperative. Schindler never expressed determination (concrete) without tempering it with fancy (wood). He was never a moralist—but his values were no less obstinate because he appeared to enjoy making his buildings. When I first saw the Kings Road house in 1941 from Pauline's garden I could not make out what was happening. The leap from concrete to clerestory to "sleeping baskets" was disorienting. When I was shown through the house an hour later the very act of movement began to slow down the images, and the forms unfolded slowly. There was an inner dynamism in the forms that involved the muscles of the body as well as the eye.

—From Esther McCoy, *Vienna to Los Angeles: Two Journeys*, Arts & Architecture Press, Santa Monica, California, 1979, p. 72.

Schindler House (R.M. Schindler, 1922),
West Hollywood, California. View of south
sleeping porch.

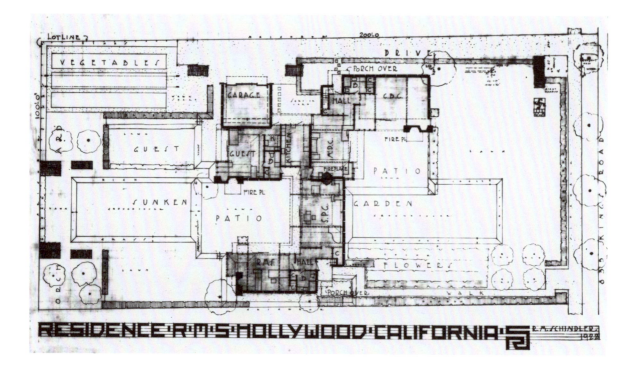

Floor plan, Schindler House (R.M. Schindler, 1922), 835 North Kings Road, West Hollywood, California. McCoy went to work in the south studio in the spring of 1944.

I saw the (Schindler) house first in 1941, when Berk and I were taken to meet Pauline, and...I couldn't understand it. It was curious and disturbing.

What Pauline said about it was poetic, but to someone who had lately worried about .032 Alclad metal at Douglas and was concerned with how things were put together, the Kings Road house was a closed world. At Pauline's I stared at the clerestories, my eye followed the transfer of loads from member to member, the transition between high roof and low roof. I tried to guess how it was done. I tried to guess why it was done. I even tried to guess how it would be drawn. I gave up questioning Pauline because the kind of questions I asked brought only assurances that structure was not the route to an aesthetic appreciation of Schindler.

Then one day Pauline told me that Schindler's only draftsman had been called into the armed service. She suggested that I apply. I'd seen Schindler only once. He was standing by his parked car kicking a tire. His thick dark hair stood out from his head in a wiry wreath (he always cut it himself), and his heavy torso was covered with a silk shirt with V-neck and no cuffs. He designed it himself.

He looked dusty and tired. I remember then that one of the reasons that people said he was not serious about architecture was that he did his own contracting. How could anyone serious about architecture spend most of the day on the job sites, one of my architect friends asked.

It took some courage to go to see him. I selected from among a dozen or so engineering drawings the two most precisely drawn and most complicated. Then I cleaned up the drawings of the house that I designed. I dressed in something that made me look serious and dependable. What did I expect? A cool dismissal. My wildest hopes were to be in the office long enough to study a set of drawings of one of his houses.

At eleven o'clock one morning I went along the row of wild Eugenias to his door, a heavy redwood swinging door with a small glazed peephole in which there was a sign reading "By appointment only." The door was ajar. I entered.

The drafting room was off a hall to the right. It was a large room lighted by windows and a clerestory on the west and thin slits of glass between the concrete panels on the east. The room was divided in the middle by a low row of shelves, with the two drafting boards at the far end. At the near end was Schindler's long desk, and back of it was a piano bench covered with a piece of cowhide. Along the west wall was a table with nothing on it but a small, portable typewriter, locked into uppercase.

Schindler was sitting at the drafting board with his back to me. When I spoke he turned around, obviously annoyed at being disturbed. I could see that I'd come at a bad time. "I wanted to ask you about a job. Maybe I should come back another time," I said.

He didn't look up from the drawing as he asked me what I had done. I took the two engineering drawings out, and said I had been two years at Douglas. He brushed them aside. "Aircraft draftsmen never know anything about the plane except the part they're working on," he said. Then, indifferently, he unrolled my drawings of the house.

I dreaded to hear what he would say about them. I hoped he would only say, "You need more experience," and I could leave. Instead he anchored them to the very dirty drawing on the board with a long flat camel's hair brush, and looked at them closely. Then he turned the pages, once even referring back to the plan on page one.

"The glass," he said. He was looking at the strip of glass I'd used in all the rooms between door height and ceiling height.

I waited. I was ready with the reason for using the glass, to bring south light into north-facing rooms, to see the trees when the curtains were pulled, and then a reason I would not have had the guts to give, to make the house fly, perhaps a hangover from working so long on the airplane wings. But he wasn't curious about why I'd used the glass, but how I'd used it. The glass was broken up with the studs.

"You could have used a longer span, you know that." That was the most encouraging thing he could have said, that I should have known something. Once pointed out, I saw it immediately, but the architectural standards book I'd been studying deigned no variations on the two-by-four stud system, sixteen inches on center.

There were other bits of advice, and with each one, I became more confident. For instance, I'd located the sofa too close to the flow of traffic. I wanted to thank him profusely and go home and rework the drawings. Then I could take them out next week to another architect.

I said in apology, "I tried to get in USC, but they discouraged me."

"The less to unlearn," he said. "Come in tomorrow at eleven, eleven to five or six. I can give you a dollar an hour."

I was stunned. He'd already helped me, and a dollar an hour was not bad. I was getting $1.30 an hour at Douglas when I quit.

—From Esther McCoy, "Schindler: A Personal Reminiscence," *L.A. Architect*, November 1987, pp. 5–9.

McCoy at her drafting board, mid-1940s.

Interior, Kallis House. While employed as a draftsperson in Schindler's office, McCoy worked on the plans for the Kallis House.

Kallis House (R.M. Schindler, 1946–48), Studio City, California. McCoy noted Schindler's unexpected and expressive use of Bouquet Canyon stone in this hillside house and studio designed for an artist.

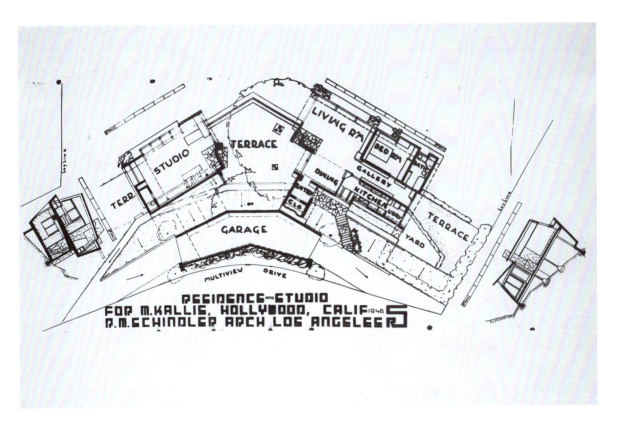

Floor plan, Kallis House. McCoy described
the angular, vaulted space as the "house with
sloping walls."

Wolfe House (R.M. Schindler, 1928), Catalina
Island, California. Schindler's design included both
house and furniture for Charles and Ethel Wolfe,
proprietors of the Wolfe School of Costume
Design. In 1956, McCoy wrote: "Plastic forms
combined with the poetic use of wood make it
one of Schindler's great achievements."

Schindler's draftsmen reunited, 1954. Left to right: Carl Sullivan, Esther McCoy, Edward Lind, Vick Santochi, and Rodney Walker. McCoy curated her first exhibition, *R.M. Schindler Retrospective*, for the Landau Art Gallery, Los Angeles, in 1954, the year after Schindler's death.

R.M. Schindler (left) and Theodore Dreiser,
Schindler's office, c. 1944.

Theodore and Helen
Richardson Dreiser, c. 1944.
In 1941, Dreiser bought
a Spanish-style house with
a large yard at 1015 North
Kings Road, West Hollywood,
California.

In 1924, McCoy was a nineteen-year-old undergraduate at the University of Michigan when she initiated a correspondence with Theodore Dreiser. The fifty-three-year-old novelist replied with terrific enthusiasm and reckless spelling:

"Your a quaint & elusive and maybe just a slightly affected person. But I like your letters. And I think I can tell you what you are going to be—eventually if not now—or right soon. A writer. You have such a flare for the visible scene & present it with so much simplicity & force. You might as well begin scribbling fort-with."

—Theodore Dreiser letter to Esther McCoy, July 9, 1924.

Living room, Dreiser Residence, c. 1944.
The angular rosewood table was designed and built by Philadelphia-based furniture maker Wharton Esherick, a friend of Dreiser's. Esherick (1887–1970), a major figure in the American Arts and Crafts movement, had created custom metal and wood furnishings for Iroki, Dreiser's eccentric country house near Mount Kisco, New York.

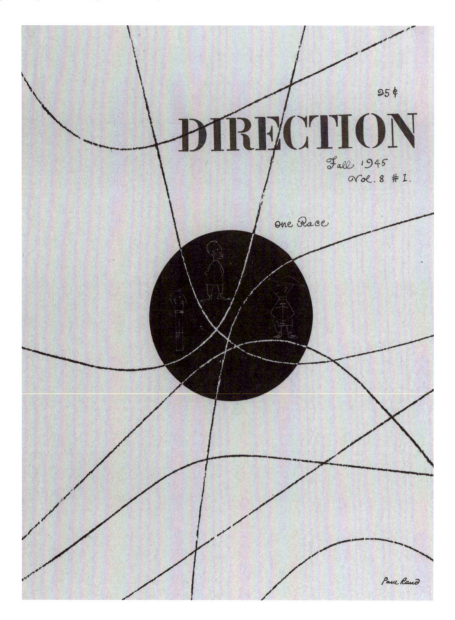

Direction vol. 8, no. 1, fall 1945. A magazine devoted to new writing and anti-fascist politics, *Direction* (1937–45) was founded with the support of Theodore Dreiser and edited by Marguerite Tjader Harris. McCoy's career as an architectural writer began when her feature "Schindler, Space Architect" was published in the fall 1945 issue.

PART 3

Speaking of Living

Frank Wilkinson (1914–2006), head of the L.A. Housing Authority and anti-poverty activist, and wife. Wilkinson managed the first integrated municipal housing (Watts, 1942) and spearheaded the Chavez Ravine public housing proposal. Investigated by California's Anti-Subversive Committee and HUAC, he was fired by the city; in 1958, he was federally incarcerated, the last person to be imprisoned during the Red Scare.

House Un-American Activities Committee (HUAC) Hearing, 1952. Screenwriter Roy Huggins testifies before the HUAC Committee, which investigated alleged subversives and Communist sympathizers during the Cold War era. The Hollywood blacklist movement, led by Ronald Reagan, then a B-movie actor and president of the Screen Actors Guild, cost 400 movie industry employees their livelihoods.

Eviction of the Vargas-Archega family from Chavez Ravine, Los Angeles, 1959. In the late 1940s, this downtown working class barrio was slated to be torn down and replaced with an integrated public housing project designed by Richard Neutra. By 1959, politicians had killed the public housing proposal; the 300-acre site was sold and developed as Dodger Stadium in 1962.

1950   Wisconsin Senator Joseph McCarthy launches his public campaign against Communism by claiming that Communist sympathizers are operating inside the government with the intent to overthrow the nation.

1950   McCoy writes the script for film *Architecture West*.

1950   McCoy joins the editorial board of *Arts & Architecture*.

1950–68   McCoy works as freelance writer for the *Los Angeles Times*.

1953   Senator McCarthy chairs the Senate Permanent Subcommittee on Investigations, which holds highly publicized hearings.

1951–55   McCoy travels to, researches, and writes about Mexico and Mexican art and architecture. The FBI keeps watch over her activities there in an effort to uncover a direct connection with American Communists in Cuernavaca.

1954   McCoy curates the *R.M. Schindler Retrospective* exhibition at the Landau Art Gallery, Los Angeles.

1956   McCoy curates the *Roots of California Contemporary Architecture* exhibition at the Los Angeles Municipal Art Department.

1957   McCoy curates the *Felix Candela* exhibition at the University of Southern California, Los Angeles.

1958   McCoy curates the *Irving Gill* exhibition at the Los Angeles County Museum of Art.

1959–68   McCoy is contributing editor to Italian periodicals *Zodiac* and *Lotus*.

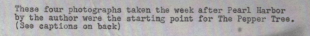

These four photographs taken the week after Pearl Harbor
by the author were the starting point for The Pepper Tree.
(See captions on back)

The pepper tree in the yard of the quarter-acre garden plot
of Yoshi and Haru Nakai, Santa Monica. Farmers of patience
crops requiring small outlay on seed and much backbreaking work.

The Nakais are in their sixties, their son Frank is 21, works
at Douglas Aircraft. They market their flowers in a model T Ford.

McCoy's storyboard for
"The Pepper Tree," c. 1942.
McCoy's novella focuses on a
second generation Japanese
American family in California
during World War II. Forced to
abandon their home and business, they are transported to a
detention camp.

The California Quarterly, autumn
1953, featuring McCoy's novella
"The Pepper Tree." Woodcut
illustration on cover by Morton
Dimondstein. Published in Los
Angeles (1951–56), CQ hoped "to
encourage writing that faces up
to its time—writers who recognize
their responsibility to deal with
reality in communicable terms."

Autumn 1953
75¢

ESTHER McCOY
The Pepper Tree

FRANK SCULLY
Portrait of an
Undesirable Alien

JAMES WYCKOFF
The Homesteader

Poems by Randall
Swingler, G.W. Brandt,
Ewart Milne, Montagu
Slater, Norman Buller,
Jack Beeching, Roy
Fuller, W. V. Evans,
Sydney Tremayne

Drawings & Engravings
by Arnold Mesches,
Morton Dimondstein,
Marion Campbell

The
California Quarterly

THE IMPORTANT HOUSE

IN the breakfast room of the new house, Mrs. Blakeley picked up the phone that was plugged in there and called a Beverly Hills number. After a pause, the operator said, "I am sorry, but all my Crestview circuits are busy." Mrs. Blakeley banged the phone down in exasperation. Her husband came through a sliding glass door from the paved terrace and walked across the pale flax carpeting as if he were stepping over eggs.

"Can't you forget it, Irene?" he asked.

"How can I forget it?" Mrs. Blakeley asked. "Wentzell's took the couch a month ago and they said it would take only two weeks to make the slipcovers."

"Well, if you can't get it, you can't," Blakeley said. It was a Saturday morning, and he was hanging around the house before going over to the club for some golf. He put his hand on one of the large sliding panels of glass that made up the whole south side of the house and gave it a playful push. It responded with a quick, easy movement that made him smile with satisfaction. He went to the built-in settee that formed an open angle around one side of the fireplace and ran his hand over the base of a lamp that was set on the plywood unit back of the settee. One end of the unit enclosed a radio and record-player.

"Lamp looks good here," he said. "Glad I bought it. Before we built the house, I never knew one lamp from another. French modern."

"It's a very nice lamp," said Mrs. Blakeley, "but what am I going to do about the couch? The photographer and Mr. Aidan are coming today."

Blakeley pulled the glass panel back and looked up at the ceiling. There was a trough along it for indirect lighting. He was an aircraft engineer, and he liked the way the house worked. They had moved into it a month ago. Morgan Aidan, the architect, had been sure they would move in two months before that. Mr. Aidan had also been sure it would cost eighteen thousand dollars, which was what they had got for the old one, but it had cost twenty-five. The Blakeleys didn't blame Mr. Aidan; they just blamed the times. Unexpected complications had come up in connection with the radiant heating; there was suddenly no copper tubing in all of Los Angeles; the pouring of the cement slab for the foundations had been delayed; and so on. Then the cabinetmaker who was assembling the built-in settees and radio unit and the built-in couch broke his arm while surf-bathing at Malibu. Mr. Aidan couldn't get someone else because the grain of the ash plywood had to be matched perfectly or the whole room would have been spoiled. It would make all the difference in the world in the way they would feel about the living room later, Mr. Aidan had maintained. It took such a long time for the cabinetmaker to recover that the built-in couch for the north end of the living room had not even been started when they moved in, and Mr. Aidan had said that since they had waited so long, they might as well wait a little longer and have some fabric woven for the couch. It was always more satisfactory having one's own fabric woven, he thought. So Mrs. Blakeley had put her old couch there in the vacant spot in the living room. It had looked very shabby in the cool chain of pastel stretching along the glass, and she had decided to get slipcovers for it. She had called Mr. Aidan, and he had sent her some swatches of color. She had taken them to Wentzell's, in Beverly Hills, and Mr. Wentzell had found some hand-blocked linen with all of Mr. Aidan's colors in it. It was a floral design—cornflowers, petunias, and some primroses. And now Mr. Aidan wanted photographs of the house—exterior and interior—and the couch wasn't back from Wentzell's.

"No use getting upset," Blakeley said. "Call the photographer and postpone it."

"Should I?"

"Why not? Everything else about the house has waited."

After several tries, she got the photographer. She told him about the couch and said, "And so, of course, we must postpone the pictures until next week." Then she listened for some time, and said, "Oh, I see," and "Oh, of course," and "No, I won't." After saying, "All right, goodbye," she hung up the phone very quietly.

"What did he say?" Blakeley asked.

"He said it was an important house," she told her husband, "and that if the pictures aren't taken today, they will miss the competition. They're to go in the *House & Garden* competition."

"They are? An important house, eh?"

Blakeley thought this over and found it pleasant. So did Mrs. Blakeley; she almost forgot about the couch.

Then the doorbell rang, and Blakeley found a man from Wentzell's standing

The New Yorker, April 17, 1948, featuring McCoy's short story "The Important House," a wry domestic drama about Mrs. Blakely and her architect-designed home. When an overbearing photographer arrives to photograph the house for a magazine, he tosses out her furniture and has his way with the interiors.

Harper's Bazaar, October 1949. McCoy's story "The Cape," first published in this issue of *Harper's Bazaar*, was republished in *The Best American Short Stories 1950*, edited by Martha Foley.

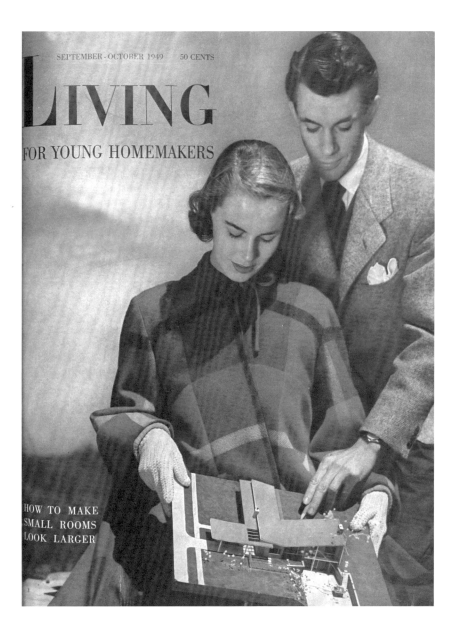

Living for Young Homemakers, September/
October 1949. A couple holding a maquette of
a prefabricated house designed by The Architect's
Collaborative, a postwar organization with a
modern, practical design philosophy, founded by
Walter Gropius in Cambridge, Massachusetts.

Lore Kingsley, "We Built a Modern House,"   ››
Living for Young Homemakers, winter
1948. *Living for Young Homemakers*, Street &
Smith Publishers (1947–59), focused on modern,
budget-minded design. Working as a contributor and architectural scout, McCoy regularly
found new houses for the magazine to feature.
She would then interview the homeowners
and ghostwrite their stories for publication.

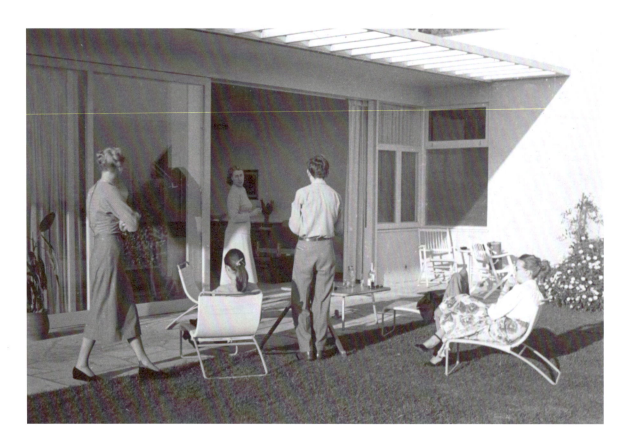

Living for Young Homemakers,
photo shoot, Kingsley House (J.R.
Davidson, 1946), Pacific Palisades,
California. McCoy in center of
photograph (standing).

ERVEN JOURDAN

70 **Outdoor living**

Lore and Joseph Kingsley and a young Kingsley on the terrace of their California house. From the terrace, they have a sweeping view of sunny lemon groves. Behind the sliding glass doors are the living-room, dining-room and breakfast room. The master bedroom, at the other end of the house, has a private garden of its own

A semi-opaque screen separates the entrance hall from the big living-room. The lack of a conventional wall increases the apparent size

By Lore Kingsley

We built a modern house

Indoor living

ERVEN JOURDAN

The entire Kingsley family consisted of just two —Joe and me—when we first decided to build a house. Joe had recently been discharged from the Army. California, where we'd always lived, was going to be our home again. We had our life pretty well planned. In our house we wanted no copper bed-warming pans with philodendron growing out of them, we wanted no cobbler's bench for a coffee-table. We weren't going to live like American colonials, French provincials or Spanish monks. No borrowed background for us. Since we were all for a modern setting, we consulted a modern architect, J. R. Davidson, and bought a lot high above the ocean at Pacific Palisades, in a subdivision well planted with ancient trees, reminders of the [Continued on page 152]

View from the terrace, showing the dining-room and a corner of the living-room. This arrangement makes entertaining large parties easy

71

JULIUS SHULMAN

By Ray Eames

« Lore Kingsley,
"We Built a
Modern House,"
*Living for Young
Homemakers,*
winter 1948.

We live in one of the newest houses in California

The apartment we live in is the direct result of a pattern of living established by our individual requirements.

A beautifully clean and simple shell was provided by Architect Richard Neutra, who designed this group of apartments. His long-developed architectural simplicities impose no style on the tenants, but leave them free to create their own surroundings through color, texture, use of area and objects and equipment needed for everyday life and activities.

In such a shell each family creates its environment without forced direction through architectural details. Our particular needs were set by a pattern of work which made the prime function of our apartment one of providing moments of calm and rest and pleasure at the beginning and end of each day. It is intended, quite selfishly and quite necessarily, for individual needs rather than to provide a setting for entertainment. Fluidity is maintained so that objects may be brought in for study and pleasure, remaining only as long as they are enjoyed or are a necessary part of work.

Since our immediate concern is the creation of form in painting, sculpture and architecture in relation to man and living, and as a direct result of the Museum of Modern Art's furniture design competition of a few years ago, in which [Continued on page 170]

Ray Eames, "We Live in One of the Newest Houses in California," *Living for Young Homemakers*, spring 1948. While living at the Strathmore Apartments (Richard J. Neutra, 1937), Westwood, California, Charles and Ray Eames developed the prototype for their molded plywood chair.

The apartment house in which the Eameses live was designed by famed modern Architect Richard J. Neutra. Built prewar, its progressive design still qualifies it as new

OFFICE OF THE LEGAL ATTACHÉ
EMBASSY OF THE UNITED STATES OF AMERICA
MEXICO CITY

Date: November 24, 1952

To: Director, FBI

From: Legat, Mexico   100-997

Subject: ESTHER McCOY
           SECURITY MATTER - C.

ReBulet August 28, 1952, which was directed to the Reverend SYDNEY J. BROWNE, Post Office Box 332, Jaffrey, New Hampshire, a copy of which was received in this office on September 8, 1952. This letter was accompanied by photostatic copies of two letters written by Reverend BROWNE to the United Nations Organization in New York City on May 8, 1952, and to the Director on August 19, 1952.

Reverend BROWNE's letter of May 8, 1952, describes an incident which occurred in Cuernavaca, Morelos, Mexico, and which indicated that one ESTHER McCOY was associating with American Communists in Cuernavaca.

CI's [   ] of known reliability, have developed considerable coverage among the American Communist group in Cuernavaca since July 7, 1952. The informants consistently spend each week-end in Cuernavaca and have furnished a voluminous amount of information concerning activities in that area. They have been specifically requested to furnish any available information concerning captioned subject but thus far have not been able to establish any connection between her and the Communist group there. The informants are continuing to follow this matter however, and the Bureau will be advised immediately of any results.

In view of the negative nature of the foregoing, no local dissemination is being made.

Pending.

GFM:LH

SE 50   396926

RECORDED-36

RECEIVED   EX. - 54

Memo from the legal division of the American Embassy in Mexico City to the FBI director, 1952. McCoy was under FBI surveillance because of her husband's membership in the Communist Party USA, and for associating with Communists at home and in Mexico.

The Bradbury Building (George H. Wyman, 1893), ››
Los Angeles, California. Photograph by Julius Shulman for McCoy's article, "A Vast Hall Full of Light," *Arts & Architecture*, April 1953. In this unpublished photograph, McCoy stands by the elevator to indicate scale.

Visionary architect R. Buckminster Fuller (left)
and John Entenza. While editor and publisher of
Arts & Architecture magazine from 1938 to 1962,
Entenza created the Case Study House program.

Esther McCoy on John
Entenza, publisher of
Arts & Architecture and
founder of the Case
Study House Program:

His goals were modest but few people affected Los Angeles more. A laissez-faire moralist, he gave the city a new and more urbane image of itself. He was too civilized to impose a program on others but nevertheless started the most successful architectural program in America: Case Study Houses. He was never regional or provincial; the first thing he did when he bought *Arts & Architecture* in 1938 was to remove the name "California" from the title. He also eliminated most of the descriptions of buildings, except the program, materials, and site solution, to accompany the plan and photographs.

Just as the magazine, after being redesigned by Herbert Matter, fit into no standard-size envelope, the contents, after being revised by Entenza with Charles and Ray Eames to include furniture, industrial design, fabrics, etc. fit no ready-made audience. As thin as a tortilla and as sleek as a Bugatti, it created a new audience from among the visually and intellectually initiated. *Arts & Architecture* was perhaps the only magazine whose appeal was almost entirely linear.

Between the sparse advertisements in the front and back pages were the regular columns. Longest were Peter Yates' music pieces, aimed at readers who listened to Bartok and Ives at the "Roof" concerts held in the small concert hall R.M. Schindler had built on top of the Yates house in Silverlake.

With its one paid editorial assistant and unpaid photographers and contributors, the magazine favored bright young architects over the middle-aged, established ones. It could not compete with the Eastern architectural journals. Instead, it was a discoverer of talent; young architects considered it a mark of great distinction to have been published in *Arts & Architecture*.

But the magazine was also a breeder of talent. As a rallying point for all the arts, it created the climate in which good work flourished. Students from Art Center went to Entenza's office with an idea for a cover and he listened. He listened to everyone, to young architects who didn't know how they were going to keep their offices open, to students from Japan or Argentina.

—From Esther McCoy, "John Entenza," *Arts & Architecture*, vol. 3., no. 3, Winter 1984, pp. 29–31.

Model of Case Study House #24 (A. Quincy Jones
and Frederick Emmons, 1961, project never built).
Photograph by Leland Y. Lee. A former assistant
to photographer Julius Shulman, Lee (1918–) has
produced his own iconic architectural photographs
for seventy years.

Esther McCoy, from
a lecture at the Los
Angeles Conservancy,
September 1984:

The 1950s had a new face.
And the dress was new.
The sex was still the same:
MALE.
The textured tweeds of the
prewar architect gave way in the
1950s to hard surfaced worsteds
and flannels.
The earth colors gave way to the
blacks and grays and gun metals.
Battleship colors.
Camouflage colors.
The hand knit tie to a narrow
black smooth heavy silk.
Black shoes.
Black socks.

It was the most educated generation of architects. They studied on the G.I. Bill. By and large they had 50 to 75 percent more education than those dropouts: Wright, Mies, Le Corbusier. And 100 percent more than the stone-carver Palladio.

The postwar generation wore wedding rings. Symbol of stability. They had experienced the Depression. They had fought in the war or worked in war plants.

They believed in the machine. They believed in decimal tolerances. They believed in the payload. Technical information was light reading. The postwar generation was least versed in the humanities, least interested in indigenous practices.

The wartime slogan had been: "Use it up/Wear it out/Make it do." By the 1950s the nation was ready for planned obsolescence. "Pull up the lines, Jack—I've got mine" was in the air. Knoll International dropped the Alvin Lustig ads because of their emphasis on economy.

...Well, that was a caricature of the high road of the 1950s. The Mies road. The Case Study House road.

There was a low road. Frank Lloyd Wright's Guggenheim Museum. And in the '50s Bruce Goff's Expressionism bloomed. In Southern California the High Road was always blending with the Low Road.... Pressed by climate and way of life, the roads merged and separated and merged again....

Some of the new figures were John Lautner, A. Quincy Jones, and Carl Maston.

There was also the group of architects who bridged the '40s and '50s—the transitional figures, all born before World War One. The ones whose reputations were established before the Second War.

I wrote about four of these in a book I called *The Second Generation*.

J.R. Davidson. Harwell Hamilton Harris. Gregory Ain. Raphael Soriano. Essentially they were one-man offices.

—From Esther McCoy, "The Second Generation," Los Angeles Conservancy Lecture, September 1984, Esther McCoy Papers, Archives of American Art, Smithsonian Institution.

Exterior, Case Study House #17
(Craig Ellwood, 1954–55), Los
Angeles, California. Case Study
House #17 was one of the largest
and most extravagant houses
in the program. Twice as large as
earlier designs, the house was
3300 square feet and the property
included a swimming pool.

Interior, kitchen pass through,
Case Study House #17.

'What I Believe . . .

ONE is tempted to compare the houses of J. R. Davidson to the novels of E. M. Forster. Both are eminently modern in spirit and bring to their work a rare nobility. They start first with people and turn upon them their quiet and penetrating attention. Davidson in his floor plans and Forster in his novels are more than recorders of life; they are interpreters.

Born in Berlin of an English father and German mother, Davidson studied architecture in London, then in Paris. He has practiced in Southern California since 1923. Davidson came to residential work after distinguishing himself in design of theaters, hotels, restaurants, shops. His houses are friendly and natural, have won awards from professional and consumer magazines, glass companies, etc. He has been honored by the Royal Institute of British Architects.

Entrance of the Gustavus Dan house illustrating belief that in residential design a plan is the most important thing. Starting with a structural idea or module may cause one to sacrifice the plan to them and if one starts instead with the plan a system of construction will emerge. The plan will reflect the life of the dwellers in it

Right, the entrance to the J. G. Schapiro house. The architect likes to avoid green next to the green of nature. Color, he feels, can become an important architectural element; he does not make his houses disappear in landscape but uses color to make the house, nature harmonize rather than matching them

This is the first in a series of statements of principles by leading Southern California architects. The last 30 years has been a time of great achievement in architecture. Behind the achievement are convictions and behind the convictions are men. Who are these men and what are some of the ideas that have controlled their design? In the following weeks Esther McCoy will present representative works of many of the architects who have contributed to our progress.

A Statement of Architectural Principles

By Esther McCoy

Left, as he shows in the living room of his own home, its size is not the determining factor in the usefulness of the living room. A successful one has space for an intimate chat, for general activity. It must not be like the railroad station through which people pass whose destination is elsewhere

Esther McCoy, "What I Believe, J.R. Davidson," *Los Angeles Times*, November 21, 1954. McCoy published an ongoing series of profiles about individual architects and their principles.

Of the living room and terrace of the Kingsley house he says, "I like to use glass on two sides of a room only so there are areas of light and areas of shadow." He does not like windows that resemble .holes punched in wall and are hard on eyes as well as ugly

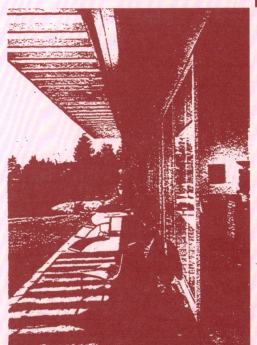

Left: the Joseph Kingsley Jr. Pacific Palisades home emphasizes the point that the concrete and steel are more suitable materials for us than any style that overemphasizes the use of wood. A return to the day of the Greene brothers for inspiration is as far from the spirit of today as is Cape Cod cottage style, according to Davidson

'What I Believe...'

Ain inspects one of his projects. He says every generation produces its Contemporary style, which appears to be the ultimate solution of obvious, clearcut problems. But our fathers' buildings seem to us rather quaint. Will our children be amused, indulgent when they inherit ours?

By Esther McCoy

GREGORY AIN is best known in the United States for the house he designed for the garden of New York's Museum of Modern Art. Californians have long known him for his contributions to the design of the small house, singly and for tracts.

Ain received a Guggenheim Fellowship in 1940 to research on structural systems which would cut cost and speed construction of the much-needed small house.

Architecture took a long time to get around to the small house, says Ain. He finds a parallel in the way medicine neglected for centuries the study of obstetrics despite the fact that childbirth was one of the greatest killers. Until only 100 years or so ago medicine considered obstetrics beneath its dignity. In our lifetime the small house has finally received the serious attention of architecture.

A resident of Los Angeles since he was 3, Ain received a degree in architecture from the University of Southern California, spent a few years in the drafting room of Richard Neutra, then, while still in his 20s, opened his own office. His first house won a national award and other honors followed for individual houses and houses for tracts. Because of his emphasis on low-maintenance homes, his plans have always appealed to women running servantless establishments. A national magazine commissioned him to design a house which proved to be something of a yardstick for the servantless houses that followed.

Although Ain designs offices and large buildings as well as individual dwellings, the most gratifying work to him has been in the design of well-planned, handsome houses for small tracts.

Screen of colored glass and a fireplace wall of ceramic tile laid to give the effect of a Chinese cloud give a severe room texture in Leo Messner's home. Ain says decorative prominence of the fireplace itself should be proportionate to the probable frequency of its use

" .... the problem today as 25 years ago is to achieve privacy without sacrificing large window areas." So Ain explains unit projects like this, built here in 1945

Julius Shulman photographs

A Statement of Architectural Principles

Yavno

"Few question advantage of large windows, but the increasing of the size of windows hasn't advanced design," says Gregory Ain

Esther McCoy, "What I Believe, Gregory Ain," *Los Angeles Times*, January 2, 1955.
An architect and educator, Ain (1908–88) developed socially conscious designs for inexpensive single-family housing and apartment buildings.

"A panoramic view from a mountain top need not be incorporated in its entirety in a living room. If too much wall gives way to glass area the dramatic value of the view may be diminished rather than heightened . . . Some contrast for the eye is needed, and furthermore the sense of the shelter of the room must be retained. Some uninterrupted blank walls are desirable to define interior space and maintain a feeling of repose"

Conservative critics have called the modern glass house a goldfish bowl and, says Ain, often are right. Windows should be placed for looking out, as in the John Wilfongs' house, left, not for looking in as they would be if facing a street

This is the second in a series of statements of principles by leading Southern California architects

Stucco is looked upon as a negative material; because of its lack of character an architect emphasizes its form

Esther McCoy, "House and the Desert Are One," *Los Angeles Times*, May 4, 1952. McCoy wrote about the Maryon Toole House (R.M. Schindler, 1946–48), Palm Springs, California. Photographs by Shirley C. Burden emphasize the stonework that Schindler described as "leopard spots."

West wall is desert rock, a protection against the strong sun. Overhang shades glass inset at right.

House and the

By Esther McCoy

WHEN R. M. Schindler designed a desert house for Miss Maryon Toole (formerly a captain in the WAC stationed in Japan) he proceeded on the theory that a house can be compact yet large in dimensions. He has combined a sense of enclosure with spaciousness.

Enclosure is achieved by the use of native stone for high west sun-break walls, with lower stone walls on the north and south.

The rock has been poured into forms with concrete and later surfaced to bring out its metallic colors. Glass is used freely for interior partitions as well for gables of the roof and in bands of windows.

Entrance is shaded by deck above two-car carport. Inside the port a storage wall holds tools, heating system and water heater.
Shirley C. Burden photos

Glass doors between living room and porch fold back to make two areas one; roof steps down to open rafters above the porch; light furniture can be moved in or out.

Desert Are One

Rock walls and glass partitions achieve compactness from without and spaciousness from within

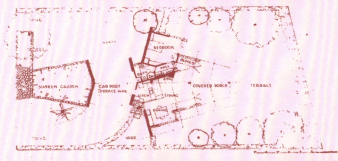

A large carport, with sun deck above, has a stone wall on the long side—the west—with the drive-through carport forming a kind of breezeway. A storage wall on the house side of the carport houses utilities as well as tools.

The entrance is at an angle from the carport, with kitchen and dining area nearby.

Various roof levels have been used to give that extra dimension to the house, which rises high on the west to permit a balcony room.

The living room moves out to become a porch, the two areas being divided by glass doors which can be folded out of the way to make the two areas one.

The fireplace, with its stain-

(Continued on Page Twenty-eight)

Stone extends into bedroom to support dressing table.

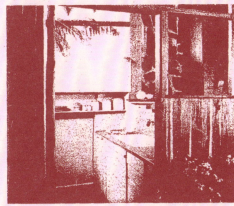

Kitchen has cupboards below counter, food bar above.

For Losers Only

The betting man's sandwich

by Esther McCoy

Marilyn Street

THE FRENCH are not ones to get excited over the sandwich, and the Escoffier Cook Book gives instructions for preparing only one, a sandwich for the races.

"In an emergency," writes Escoffier or his editor, "it answers the purpose of a meal" and "is liked by racing people."

So if you number yourself among the racing set and expect an emergency at the track . . .

Required:
1 loaf of bread
1 thick steak
  Grated horse-radish and mustard
  Blotting paper
1 letter press
1 shoe box
1 emergency

Ready? Got your letter press handy? All right, now cut the ends off the loaf of bread, slit it lengthwise and butter it. While you're doing this, grill a thick steak. When that's done, season it with salt and pepper and sprinkle grated horse-radish and mustard over it. Now lay it between the pieces of bread and bind the whole thing together as for a galantine.

You don't know what a galantine is? Then go out and buy an Escoffier Cook Book. You should have had one long ago. Nine-tenths of all cookbooks simply paraphrase Escoffier, taking him out of his scholarly style and putting him into the vulgate which we can better comprehend.

You'll have only one problem with Escoffier and that's because you have only 10 fingers. The wisest thing is to start off with a simple three-finger recipe. For example, take veal sweetbreads Richelieu.

The first sentence of the recipe refers you to Recipe 1221 for ris de veau bonne maman, which in turn sends you to Recipe 248, a dissertation on the braising of white meats, which hurries you on to Recipe 9 on the preparation of brown veal stock, which refers you to Recipe 10 (on the same page, so you don't need another finger) for white veal stock.

Not until you can handle a nine-finger recipe do you receive your Escoffier diploma.

Well, it's almost time for the first race, so back to the sandwich. After you've tied your sandwich together, wrap it in several sheets of blotting paper and place it under a letter press. "Leave the sandwich thus for one-half hour," says the Escoffier.

Don't think that you can now start putting on your coat. The screw of the letter press has to be gradually tightened. Keep your mind on the sandwich and the emergency. At the end of the half-hour the sandwich has become saturated with meat juice. So wrap it in waxed paper and place it in a shoe box.

You don't have a shoe box? What a pity! Ask your nearest bookie.

Esther McCoy, "The Betting Man's Sandwich," *Los Angeles Times*, September 21, 1958. From 1950 to 1968, McCoy was a freelance contributor to the *Los Angeles Times*. Her articles ranged from architectural profiles and design stories to personal essays and travel pieces.

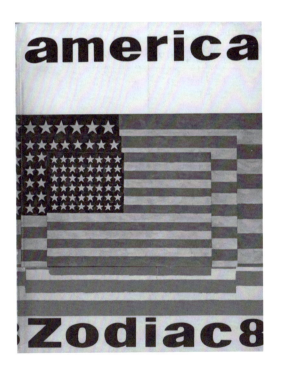

Zodiac 8, "America," 1961. Cover: *Three Flags* by Jasper Johns. From 1959 to 1968, McCoy was a contributing editor at *Zodiac*, a twice-yearly publication edited by art critic Bruno Alfieri and produced under the auspices of C. Olivetti & Co.

Exterior, Schindler House (R.M. Schindler, 1922),
West Hollywood, California. This undated photo-
graph by Esther McCoy appeared in the first
edition of Robert Winter and David Gebhard's
A Guide to Architecture in Southern California,
Los Angeles County Museum of Art, 1965.
Schindler, as McCoy later noted, preferred—like
T.S. Eliot and H.L. Mencken—to be known by his
initials; he disliked the name Rudolf, was generally
called Michael, and signed everything "R.M.S."

PART 4

The Past Teaches the Present

Aerial photo of the Dodge House (Irving Gill, 1916) West Hollywood, California after the zoning change from R-1 to R-4, 1963.

Student protest at the Federal Building as the House Un-American Activities Committee met to investigate Communist activities in Los Angeles, 1962.

Police searching young men for weapons in Watts during the riots of 1965. The Watts Riots began with a traffic stop and ended six days later with thirty-four dead, one thousand injured, nearly four thousand arrested, and block after block of destroyed buildings. The riots were widely attributed to the deep sense of despair the inner-city community felt in response to high unemployment, inadequate housing, substandard schools, police brutality, and racism.

Demolition of the Dodge House (Irving Gill, 1916), 1970.

1960	McCoy publishes *Five California Architects* (New York: Reinhold), which becomes an instant classic on California architecture.
1960	McCoy publishes *Richard Neutra* (New York: G. Braziller).
1962	Death of Berkeley Greene Tobey.
1962	McCoy publishes *Modern California Houses: Case Study Houses* (New York: Reinhold) (reprinted as *Case Study Houses* [Los Angeles: Hennessey and Ingalls, 1978]).
1963	Zoning on Kings Road is changed from R-1 to R-4, paving the way for the demolition of single-family dwellings and the construction of condominiums.
1963	McCoy becomes active in an effort to save the Dodge House (Irving Gill, 1916).
1965	Five days of riots erupt in the Watts neighborhood of Los Angeles.
1965–66	McCoy writes and produces the film *Dodge House, 1916*.
1965–68	McCoy becomes a lecturer in the School of Architecture and Urban Planning, University of California, Los Angeles.
1967	McCoy curates the *Ten Italian Architects* exhibition, Los Angeles County Museum of Art.
1968	McCoy publishes *Craig Ellwood* (New York: Walker).
1969–89	McCoy is contributing editor of *Progressive Architecture* and *Architectural Forum*.
1970	Dodge House is demolished.
1979	McCoy publishes *Vienna to Los Angeles: Two Journeys* (Santa Monica, California: Arts & Architecture Press).
1984	McCoy publishes *The Second Generation* (Salt Lake City, Utah: Peregrine Smith Books).
1989	McCoy contributes a catalog essay for the *Blueprints for Modern Living: History and Legacy of the Case Study House* exhibition at the Museum of Contemporary Art, Los Angeles.
1989	McCoy dies in Santa Monica, California, on December 30.

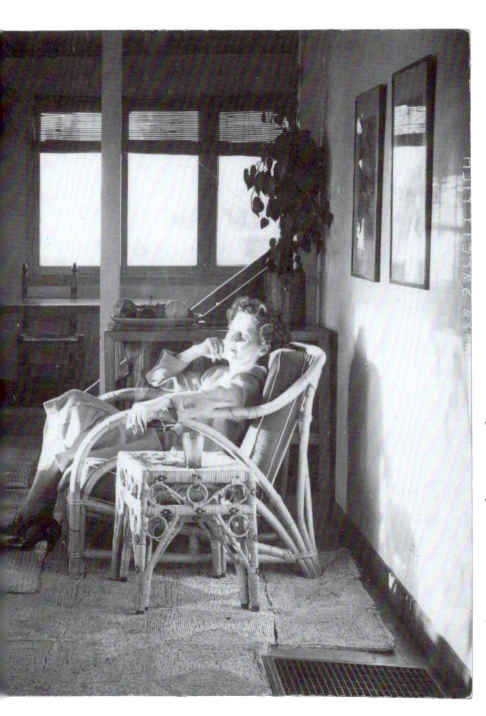

Esther McCoy (left) and her mother, Katie McCoy, visiting Santa Monica, California, from Coffeyville, Kansas, c. 1947. "My mother's reading started about 5 in the morning with the newspaper, which she always opened at the editorial page," wrote McCoy in 1958. "Fiction reading was a chore to her, but she dearly loved a president's speech. Once, in a *New Yorker* story of mine, a character based loosely on my mother was reading a Supreme Court minority report early one morning in bed. The editors changed it to a weather report. My mother never gave a rap for the weather; she goes by seasons."

FIVE CALIFORNIA ARCHITECTS

ESTHER McCOY

GREENE & GREENE

MAYBECK

SCHINDLER

GILL

About the Author

Very few people have a better background and knowledge of California architecture than Esther McCoy.

Born in Santa Monica, California, she worked in Schindler's office, personally interviewed Maybeck at two points in his career, knew Gill's nephew (also an architect) and over the years gathered a wealth of material on the Greene brothers.

Her writing and research background is also impressive. She has written fiction for The New Yorker and Harper's Bazaar and contributed numerous articles on California and Mexican architecture to architectural magazines, as well as literary quarterlies.

The catalogs for the exhibit "Roots of California Contemporary Architecture" and "The Irving Gill Show" were prepared by Mrs. McCoy. She also wrote the script for the film "Architecture West."

As a member of the Editorial Advisory Board of the celebrated West Coast magazine "Arts & Architecture" she is constantly aware of new developments in California architecture. Her many articles in the *Los Angeles Times Home Magazine* have done much to create interest in architecture among the general public.

Mr. Randell L. Makinson, who contributed the chapter on Greene and Greene, is a designer and an instructor at the University of Southern California.

REINHOLD PUBLISHING CORPORATION

Esther McCoy, *Five California Architects*, Reinhold Publishing, New York, 1960. In remarkably lucid prose, McCoy articulated the work of Irving Gill, Bernard Maybeck, R.M. Schindler, and brothers Charles and Henry Greene (in a chapter by Randell Makinson) and delivered an unprecedented look at American modernist architecture and its distinctly West Coast roots.

Reyner Banham
on *Five California
Architects:*

"Until about 1960, the rest of the world had practically no idea at all about architecture in California, what it was like, how good it was, if it even existed. Through the fifties the situation had been mending slowly because *Arts & Architecture*, a Los Angeles-based monthly, had been publishing the work of outstanding modern California architects like Richard Neutra and a whole brilliant younger generation of Angelenos: Charles and Ray Eames, Pierre Koenig, Craig Ellwood and so forth—and publishing it so stylishly under the editorship of John Entenza that the world was beginning to take notice. Then this extraordinary book came out in 1960, and—suddenly—California architecture had heroes, history and character.

It was called *Five California Architects*; it described the careers of earlier architects whose works are now objects of international pilgrimage but were then hardly names to most of us: Charles and Henry Greene, Irving Gill, Bernard Maybeck, R.M. Schindler. The author, Esther McCoy, wasn't even a name outside California, barely known in Los Angeles, where she lived. But it was clear that she knew her stuff, was a real scholar, though she seemed to belong to no known academic faction or school of thought, and could write—the book was so damned readable it was in a different league than most architectural literature."

—From Reyner Banham, "The Founding Mother," *Angeles*, March 1984.

Walter L. Dodge House (Irving J. Gill, 1916, demolished 1970).
Photograph by Marvin Rand. Gill's masterwork, the Dodge
House, at 950 North Kings Road in West Hollywood, California,
was widely regarded as the first fully modernist residence in the
West. When McCoy met Rand in 1952, he had just graduated
from Art Center College of Design. While working with McCoy,
Rand documented many of Gill's buildings.

Dodge House. "On the street side—Kings Road,"
McCoy noted of the Dodge House, "it appeared
to be a pure concrete box—and it *was* pure. On
the front, there was a raised porch extending
around to the north...."

Gardens, Dodge House.

Esther McCoy on
the Dodge House:

The preliminary plans were dated August 10, 1914, but the house was not finished until 1916. This was due to the extraordinary amount of detailing and, perhaps, also to the war in Europe. The building covered 6,500 square feet, and there were over 1,100 square feet of porches. Compared to the approximate rectangle of most of Gill's houses, the plan was sprawling, with a porch cutting a U into the north side and a walled court taking a corner from the south. The court, reached through the French doors of the dining room and breakfast room, served as an unroofed living area. The interweaving of inner and outer space was well suited to living needs; and the floor plan was unusually fluid.

The 300-square-foot entrance hall was one of Gill's most beautiful rooms. The walls were entirely paneled in boards of Honduras mahogany, so meticulously matched that they gave the impression of a single slab of richly patterned wood. Although, today, plywoods produced by machine methods achieve a similar effect, the character of the room lay deeper than in the fine craftsmanship or the historical importance of the flushed detailing.

It was the light from the stairwell that gave the room much of its beauty. Entering through 10-foot-high windows, which filled the north wall, the light extended the upper space and determined the shape of the room. It warmed the wood to life, and emphasized the chasteness of the balustrade and the fine joinery of the handrail.

[...]

In this reinforced concrete house, Gill accomplished what he had started out to do in 1908, when he first began his study of concrete construction as an art. It was to bring concrete to the architectural importance of stone.

The Dodge house was not only a fulfillment, it was also a promise of change. The plan was freer than usual and the elevations were varied, puzzlingly so upon first encounter. The south elevation with its rhythm of arches did not predict the severe west elevation. The north side, with its deeply inset porch and the play of roof stack forms against the masses, showed a preoccupation with depth.

The plan spread out in ranch-like fashion to include a raised swimming pool and garage. The romantic gardens to the north, with their fountains and loggia, gave way on the east to propagating sheds, a corral and pergolas in wooded settings.

In the early forties, Theodore Dreiser lived across the street from the Dodge house and could often be seen strolling through the neglected grounds; his last book contains a description of a crumbling pergola overrun with vines.

—From Esther McCoy, *Five California Architects* (New York: Reinhold, 1960).

Dodge House demolition, 1970. *Los Angeles Herald Examiner*, February 10, 1970.

Dodge House demolition, February 10, 1970.
McCoy was quoted in the *Los Angeles Times*:
"Losing the Dodge House is like seeing a Braque
kicked down the street.…"

Mrs. Harry Reif, a neighbor, on witnessing the Dodge House demolition:

"I went out in the morning and when I came back two hours later the wrecking crew was there. They beat it and beat it and it wouldn't go down. It was like an animal being beaten. They kept beating and beating and it finally cracked up. The trees didn't want to go either but they beat them until by late afternoon everything was gone. And they left it there. After a few weeks the neighbors complained about the rubble being left and then one morning they took it away and now nothing is left."

—From a note in the Esther McCoy Papers, Archives of American Art, Smithsonian Institution.

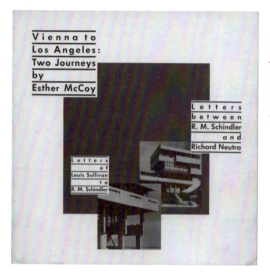

Esther McCoy, *Vienna to Los Angeles: Two Journeys*, Arts & Architecture Press, Santa Monica, California, 1979. McCoy presents and considers the correspondences, both epistolary and ideological, between Austrian émigré architects R.M. Schindler and Richard Neutra.

Esther McCoy on the Lovell Beach House (R.M. Schindler, 1925–26):

Leah [Press Lovell] said of the beach house, "Philip [Lovell] wanted it first on the palisades but the children were five and two and six months so the beach seemed better. We got two lots on 13th Street across from the courts where we played tennis."

"There was a pubic walk past the lots to the beach," and that was why Schindler raised the house above the ground. The living room is on the second floor and the ground under it is a playground for the children. But labor gave him trouble." The site was remote in 1925 and some of the crew camped in tents on the beach. "Schindler would drive out and the men would be doing things wrong and he would make them tear it out."

The glass wall facing the ocean also caused trouble. "I wanted steel windows but Schindler loved wood. Thirty or forty of the panels in the big window sagged. The wood was pre-milled and it didn't fit well, and it was always being repainted because of the salt air. On the positive side, Schindler paid attention to our way of living and adjusted to it, which Neutra didn't. Private places for nude sunbathing on the roof. But the wind blew the rain into the sleeping porches. It was right over the public walk and I could lie in bed in the morning and hear the conversations of people walking to the beach. They called it the upside down house. They thought it was crazy. So did the loan companies. I was never able to get a loan on any house I built. I've always been a minority in everything. There were other modern houses around but you couldn't see them for all the Mission and Moorish styles. So I did some experimenting."

Schindler had pierced the stucco rail of the sleeping porch with small slots at bed height, so Lovell saw as well as heard the detractors of the house. This got to be an annoyance, so he called in Schindler to see what could be done. The bedrooms were in a line along the sleeping porch, separated from it by glass and wood screen walls; Schindler moved the screens forward and cut them to fit the space above the rail. He must have done it reluctantly because with the rail and screens on the same plane there was no longer the sense of hollowed-out space he had achieved on the ground level. But like many of Schindler's solutions it was ingenious and simple.

Lovell may have wanted to experiment but the penalties were a constant source of annoyance. His letters to Schindler show a growing impatience. The man who did the "woodstone" work for the floors performed badly, and Schindler wrote listing the flaws (when patching, the colors didn't match, etc.), then dismissed him and enclosed a short check. The man presented the balance of the bill to Lovell who paid it and scolded Schindler, whereupon Schindler wrote that if he was to get quality work he must make the decisions about the payment of bills. Lovell then wrote that the man claimed the fault was Schindler's for having changed the plans; Schindler denied that the plans had been changed and asked haughtily how Lovell could believe he would be so low as to take advantage of a workman. So it went. The idea for spraying on the paint (then new) didn't work, and Schindler reprimanded the painter for not finishing with brush what the spray had missed, and for spattering paint over the floors.

The furniture was another trial.

"RMS wanted everything in the house to blend together," Mrs. Lovell said. "The bed frames were the same design as the windows. I remember that the wood had the look of seaweed. The leftover wood was cut up to make the stools and the long sofa in the living room. He gave Maria Kipp [a textile designer] yards and yards of cheese cloth and monk's cloth to dye a golden yellow for the curtains and rust for the cover for the sofa. When he finished, everything looked as if it belonged there."

"The costs kept going up," Lovell said. (The beach house, planned originally as a smaller structure, was estimated at $8,000; as the plan grew the estimate went to $11,000, then to around $15,000. Problems in building raised the cost to around $18,000, with fee and Schindler's charge for transportation to the site making a total of $21,000. The cost of the furniture was $1,600.) Lovell continued, "The beach house ran 30 percent above the estimates, but then the town house [Lovell Health House by Richard J. Neutra, 1929] ran a hundred percent over. Even though Bethlehem Steel gave us a substantial reduction on the steel so we would open the house to the public. We got 30,000 feet of steel for $15,000. It was a serious, dignified house but I didn't belong there. The plan was too Germanic—the children and housekeeper getting the worst, their rooms on the north were cold, and the master getting the best, all the sun. No possibility for nude sunbathing. No possibility for sleeping in the open. We screened in a porch to sleep on but the beds were twelve inches apart. [Neutra] called it Health House but RMS gave us more along those lines. And RMS would drive down to the beach with his carpenter when we wanted something changed or repaired. He never made us feel that we were interfering with a work of art."

—From Esther McCoy, *Vienna to Los Angeles: Two Journeys* (Santa Monica, California: Arts & Architecture Press, 1979).

Exterior, Lovell Beach House (R.M. Schindler, ››
1925–26). When Italian architect Giancarlo de Carlo first visited the Lovell Beach House with McCoy, he swore that he had seen it with her before, quoting her vibrant description from *Five California Architects*.

Lovell Beach House (R.M. Schindler, 1925–26),
Newport Beach, California. Schindler designed
this summer residence for the Lovell family.
Dr. Phillip Lovell, a naturopath practitioner and
newspaper columnist, and Leah Press Lovell, a
progressive educator, were part of Los Angeles's
early avant-garde community.

Interior, Lovell Beach House. "In the beach house," wrote McCoy, "Schindler developed living space inside five free-standing concrete frames cast in the form of square figure eights."

Lovell Health House (Richard J. Neutra, 1929), Los Angeles, California. Neutra's brilliant design for the Lovell family's house in town is recognized as one of "the greatest monuments of International Style in Southern California."

Esther McCoy, *Richard Neutra*, George
Braziller, Inc., New York, 1960. Published as
part of Braziller's Masters of World Architecture
Series, McCoy's study of Neutra proved
personally problematic yet was critically well
received. *The Saturday Review* proclaimed:
"Richard Neutra, a man of human proportions,
is sensitively delineated in the sketch drawn by
a literary artist, Esther McCoy."

Esther McCoy, *Modern California Houses: Case Study Houses, 1945–1962*, Reinhold Publishing, New York, 1962. Reprinted by Hennessey and Ingalls, Santa Monica, California, 1978. McCoy described the Case Study House program of *Arts & Architecture* magazine as "an attempt to produce prototypes of good small modern houses at the end of the Second World War."

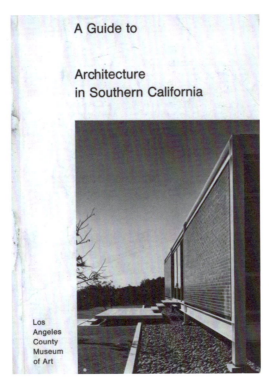

A Guide to

Architecture
in Southern California

Los
Angeles
County
Museum
of Art

David Gebhard and Robert Winter, *A Guide to Architecture in Southern California*, Los Angeles County Museum of Art, 1965. Gebhard and Winter declare: "Our present awareness of Southern California architectural heritage has been due almost to a one-woman crusade upon the part of the critic and historian, Esther McCoy."

Esther McCoy, *Ten Italian Architects*, catalog
for an exhibition organized by the Los Angeles
County Museum of Art under the direction of
Esther McCoy, Los Angeles, 1967. It featured the
work of Franco Albini and Franca Helg, Ludovico
B. di Belgiojoso, Enrico Peressutti and Ernesto
N. Rogers, Giancarlo de Carlo, Ignazio Gardella,
Angelo Mangiarotti, Giovanni Michelucci,
Alberto Rosselli, Carlo Scarpa, Gino Valle, and
Vittoriano Viganò. The exhibition's handsome
catalog and installation were designed by
John and Marilyn Neuhart.

Blueprints for Modern Living: History and Legacy of the Case Study Houses, edited by Elizabeth A. T. Smith, Museum of Contemporary Art, Los Angeles, 1989. *Blueprints for Modern Living* was a landmark exhibition about the Case Study House program's history and ongoing influence.

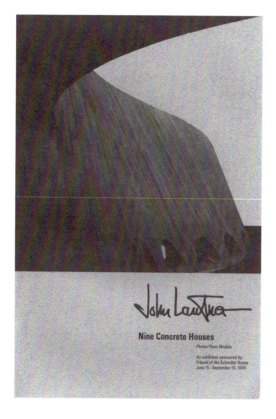

Esther McCoy, *Nine Concrete Houses*,
catalog for John Lautner exhibition,
June 14–September 15, 1985, R.M. Schindler
House, West Hollywood, California.
"…His houses are thorny with ideas, ideas
that wake up the eye and astonish the mind,"
observed McCoy in "The Ultimate Climes
of John Lautner," her essay written to accompany the Lautner exhibition.

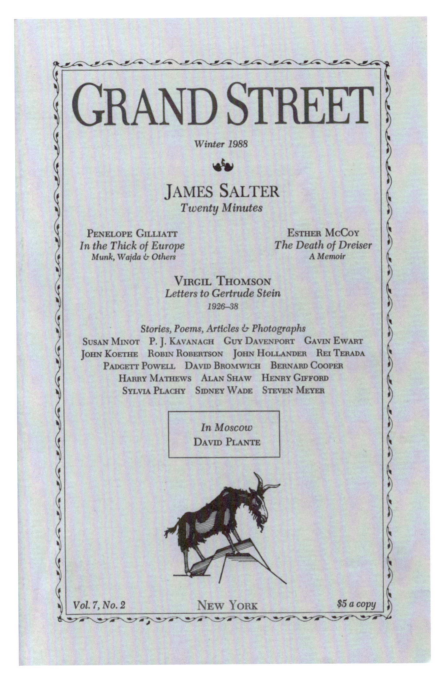

GRAND STREET

Winter 1988

JAMES SALTER
Twenty Minutes

PENELOPE GILLIATT
In the Thick of Europe
Munk, Wajda & Others

ESTHER McCOY
The Death of Dreiser
A Memoir

VIRGIL THOMSON
Letters to Gertrude Stein
1926–38

Stories, Poems, Articles & Photographs
SUSAN MINOT   P. J. KAVANAGH   GUY DAVENPORT   GAVIN EWART
JOHN KOETHE   ROBIN ROBERTSON   JOHN HOLLANDER   REI TERADA
PADGETT POWELL   DAVID BROMWICH   BERNARD COOPER
HARRY MATHEWS   ALAN SHAW   HENRY GIFFORD
SYLVIA PLACHY   SIDNEY WADE   STEVEN MEYER

In Moscow
DAVID PLANTE

Vol. 7, No. 2   NEW YORK   *$5 a copy*

Esther McCoy, "The Death of Dreiser: A Memoir,"
Grand Street, vol. 7, no. 2, winter 1988. During
the 1980s, the literary quarterly *Grand Street*
published McCoy's memoirs about 1920s
Greenwich Village, the Great Crash, and Theodore
Dreiser. Ben Sonnenberg, the magazine's founding
editor, admired McCoy's writing for its strength,
redolent atmosphere, and "wonderful population."

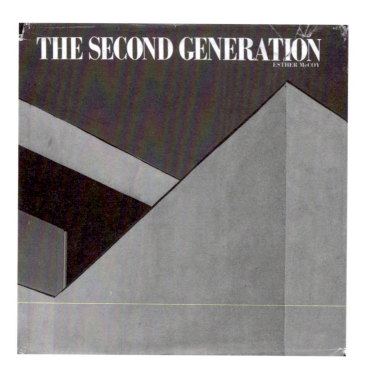

Esther McCoy, *The Second Generation*, Peregrine
Smith, Salt Lake City, Utah, 1984. McCoy's book
focused on how modernist architecture continued
to evolve and expand in Southern California.
The featured architects were J.R. Davidson,
Harwell Hamilton Harris, Gregory Ain, and
Raphael Soriano.

Birtcher House (Harwell Hamilton Harris, 1942), Los Angeles, California. Photograph by Man Ray. In *The Second Generation*, McCoy describes Man Ray's knack for blending together classicism and surrealist humor: "Several of Harris's houses were photographed by Man Ray, among them the Birtcher house. His eye found the hard forms; he freed a house from nature and it stood isolated, as if in the strong shadowless light of Greece.… Man Ray's low, sleek sports car was often parked in the foreground, another strong shape. A close-up of the car would have shown the mouse-trap dangling inside the rear window—a parody of baby's booties that graced car windows in the 1940s."

"She read floor plans like lines of a palm, interpreting social history through the evolution of the layout. She built her arguments from hard facts, always revealed in transparent prose.

She cropped her white hair short. She smoked like a fireman; she took her Bloody Marys with gin. She loved greatly and was greatly loved. She was radiant."

—Joseph Giovannini, *Progressive Architecture*, February 1990.

« Esther McCoy at work, Santa Monica, California, c. 1985.

Interview with Esther McCoy by
Makoto Shin Watanabe, 1984

Makoto Shin Watanabe: When and how did you become interested in Los Angeles modern architecture?

Esther McCoy: I was very interested in architecture. During the war I had been working as an engineering draftsman on a postwar plane, the C-74 Globemaster, detailing wings and other parts of the plane. I worked there two years and decided to study architecture. My application was discouraged at the University of Southern California so I got a job instead, with [R.M.] Schindler, who happened to need someone. He always had very few people in his office. He preferred people who had not worked in other offices.

MSW: You mean ones who didn't have professional experience in other offices?

EM: Yes, especially in big offices. He liked students and it was very hard for him to get anyone then because everyone was going into the service. When I went into the office I was the only draftsman.

MSW: When was this?

EM: I think it was about March 1944. He was doing a great deal of work then, many houses. He was also working on the last of the interiors of Bethlehem Baptist Church [1944]. And the Laurelwood Apartments [1946–49], which was a long time on the boards. I worked on these and on two or three houses. Before the war he had a lot of time for each job because there was so little work during the Depression, in the thirties. In the forties he took everything and was working

very hard. He usually made a rough plan in ⅛" = 1'0"
scale, and I developed it in ¼" = 1'0" scale. I wrote the
first article about him while I was there, for a magazine
called *Direction*.

EM: So you were working for Schindler during the
period when he was going into a more personal regional
or expressionistic style.

EM: I would not say regional, because others were very
much influenced by the region.

MSW: Could you name some of the Schindler houses
you were involved in?

EM: Let's see…Toole House [1946–48], that was in Palm
Desert, the Laurelwood Apartments, the Felix Pres-
burger House [1945–47] in North Hollywood, remodeling for Westby, and the Tischler House [1949–50]. I left
Schindler's office but I went back two or three times
when he needed help. During one of those times, I
worked on the Tischler House.

MSW: You were in his office from 1944 until when?

EM: May have been 1944 to 1947, with one break.
I may have gone back in 1948 or 1949 for a couple
of weeks.

MSW: After you'd started writing about California
modern architecture.

EM: Yes. There was so much interesting work being
built in Los Angeles, much more than any place else, so
magazines would ask me to write about them.

MSW: You mean that Los Angeles was a booming city in
the 1940s?

EM: Yes. The editors knew the architects from the
prewar days, and then there were young postwar
architects. When I was in Schindler's office, there
were many unanswered requests from publications for
his work. He hadn't had anything photographed for

a number of years so I urged him to get the late work photographed. Schindler didn't like photographers much. He would crop the photographs and come out with some little detail.

MSW: I wanted to ask you about the conditions of Los Angeles, in terms of the architects, in the 1940s.

EM: The volume of building was great because everyone was building a great deal. There was so little building in the 1930s, and the increase in population [in the 1940s] made it absolutely necessary.

MSW: I see. It was not only the modernists, but all the people.

EM: Yes, everyone.

MSW: Before we go into the 1940s or 1950s, I'd like to ask you about Schindler's clients and [his wife] Pauline Schindler. What was your impression of them? The reason I ask is that I have an impression that Schindler and his clients made up an avant-garde cultural circle.

EM: They were either in the avant-garde in the arts or left wing politically. Clients were interested in reforms in teaching or other fields. The Schindlers attracted avant-garde friends in music, dance, arts, and photography. I knew Pauline very well and liked her. She was a very difficult woman, but I was very fond of her.

MSW: When you say very difficult, in what sense?

EM: Well, she was haughty. She didn't get on too well with people, as a whole. But she also had something else. She had a great sense of literary style, which few had.

MSW: How was Neutra during that period? Did he come to visit Schindler once in a while?

EM: Never, from the time they broke up.

MSW: When did this happen?

EM: Well, it was when Neutra came back from Europe [1930]. That's in *Vienna to Los Angeles* [Santa Monica: Arts & Architecture, 1979]. Schindler did not want to see him.

MSW: What was your impression of Neutra?

EM: I like Neutra's work very much. He was a man who was driven. His ambitions were boundless. He wasn't a pleasant man at all, very childish.

MSW: It seems to me that both of them, Schindler and Neutra...their styles gradually changed from the International Style into more personal style. Is there any reason for this?

EM: The Kings Road house [Schindler House (R.M. Schindler, 1922)] was not International Style at all.

MSW: For example, Lovell Beach House [R.M. Schindler, 1925–26], although it was not the International Style, has something similar to what other people were doing in Europe.

EM: Lovell Beach House? I do not think that was similar to anything I know of.

MSW: Well, in terms of the concept of the building, the Lovell Health House by Neutra [1929] is a more straight response to the European modern movement. Maybe, the term "International Style" is not appropriate.

EM: The cubistic, yes, if you want to call that "International."

MSW: So, you think Schindler's was a more personal style from the beginning?

EM: I don't know quite what personal means. His style varied, I wouldn't call it international. It's the terms I object to: international versus personal.

MSW: Maybe then we should just use a very vague definition as "modern." His was very modern in that sense. And Neutra, with a little difference, was also pursuing modernism. In the case of Schindler, typically in work like the Tischler House, he changed his style. And Neutra gradually changed his style into the style of the Kaufmann House [1946].

EM: Well, I think Schindler changed his style twice. And each time it came out of the economy. Schindler's first period was a concrete period; he wanted to build mainly in concrete. And then, with the Depression, concrete was too costly. And he went to cubic forms that were easy to make with plaster walls. The second style change came when the cost of craftsmen became so high—the wages of the plasterer.

MSW: So that was around 1945.

EM: From 1945 to1950, mainly. And it went on into the early 1950s. The plastering happened to be the biggest cost of construction, in time as well as dollars.

MSW: That's why Schindler had to look for some other style?

EM: Yes. That led to a change in the roof because he could do two things at once: putting in a grooved planking roof that also served as a base for nailing the composition roofing to. It saved the cost of plastering the ceiling. It also led to the more expressive roof because you couldn't have heavy planking. And you could not have it in long spans.

MSW: That's why he started using the pitched roof.

EM: That also led to screen walls, which were also typical of his style in the 1950s. It wasn't very successful in some ways, but it was a prediction of what would have been a new style.

MSW: What do you think caused the change in Neutra's style? You were saying in Schindler's case it was the economy that almost forced him to change in style and look for something else.

EM: Not almost—it did. Yes, it definitely did.

MSW: Do you think that it was the same in Neutra's case?

EM: In a larger sense, but not in the smaller things because Neutra didn't strive for such low cost.

MSW: Yes, that was the point I was going to make. Because it seems to me that Neutra's postwar houses were more expensive, using the huge glass screens, and using more expensive materials, like stone walls.

EM: True. Schindler did not like the soft pink stone and Arizona flagstone that Neutra used. Schindler used a stone in the Toole House, in Palm Desert, that he called leopard spots. Then he also had a rougher stone, a Bouquet Canyon stone, he used in other houses because he did not like pastel stone. If he were going to use stone, he wanted it to be very expressive.

MSW: Now I want to talk about the architects that you profile in *The Second Generation* [Salt Lake City: Peregine Smith, 1984]. Could you give some brief introduction to those people: [J.R.] Davidson, [Harwell Hamilton] Harris, [Gregory] Ain, and [Raphael] Soriano.

EM: Second generation is a misnomer in this respect; Davidson was older than Neutra. He arrived in California before Neutra. He's categorized there because there is no other convenient place to put him, and I wanted to write about him. Ain, Harris, and Soriano were in the Neutra office so they are definitely second generation. They stem from Neutra, but they did not follow him for long.

MSW: Those three—Harris, Ain, and Soriano—are obviously a second generation. So let's talk about Davidson just for a while. What was Davidson's position in the 1930s? In your book you say he never had to look for clients. He had a lot of jobs, lots of shops, even in the Depression period.

EM: He was not aggressive. There were always jobs of some sort. They weren't large jobs and they weren't highly paid.

MSW: Was he able to get those commissions from his friends or from German émigrés?

EM: It was by word of mouth. Many clients came from the art world, many came from the films; even the Thomas Mann House [J.R. Davidson, 1941] came through the films. The clients of the two houses in the Palisades, the Kingsleys, were German refugees.

MSW: And we should look at the younger three people: Harris, Ain, and Soriano.

EM: Harris comes more out of the wood tradition of inland California.

MSW: That's right. He's different from the other two. It also seems to me that Harris was able to use different styles than the others.

EM: Yes, he was and he changed. He went into sort of a FLW [Frank Lloyd Wright] Romanza period in Texas.

MSW: Was he considered a modernist?

EM: No, not really.

MSW: He's more like the Bay Area style? Or, how can you describe him, or his style?

EM: Well, I think they felt that he was carrying on from Greene and Greene.

MSW: So, regional.

EM: Yes. However, he did do these houses of stud and plaster here in Southern California, and they were always closer to Wright than his houses of wood. I happen to like Harris's wood houses immensely—the Wyle House [1948] is one of my favorites and then of course the Havens House [1940–41] is wonderful.

MSW: So maybe he was unique because he was able to use those different styles.

EM: Yes.

MSW: We should now talk about his colleagues: Soriano and Ain. Maybe we should start with Ain. Something that surprises me is that Ain started very young and was very active in the 1930s. Was it because of the Depression?

EM: He built less and less after he began teaching. He enjoyed teaching.

MSW: What do you think of Ain and his work?

EM: It's very crisp. I like those two-by-fours that are painted white and frame things. It is so neatly packaged in these ribbons of white-painted two-by-fours. He did so much with those, it became a sort of a design symbol for him.

MSW: So, although he worked for Neutra for some period, was Ain more influenced by Schindler?

EM: In a way, yes. But he took a great deal from Neutra, more than he would admit, I'm sure. Neutra's buildings were very well built, and so were Ain's. Schindler's were not well built; they were fragile, to get them up cheaply.

MSW: You say that the Dunsmuir Flats [1937] is one of Ain's best works.

EM: Yes, I do. It's strange, you know, it's so different from one side to the other and he's always resented it not being shown from the garden side. The north side is right out of Neutra, right out of the International Style. And that first Ain house, the Edwards House [1936], is very Schindlerian.

MSW: So in that period, say the late 1930s, if you were a young architect you'd be using Schindler and Neutra as sort of Cartesian coordinate points of references.

EM: Yes, true. Absolutely true. And there wasn't anything else.

MSW: There was no one else?

EM: Well, the Europeans, I mean. Ain was always closer to the Europeans than he was to Americans because of his background, and then Soriano was very close to the Europeans, too.

MSW: What was the influence of Frank Lloyd Wright on the younger generation?

EM: Well, there was a period during the 1950s in Los Angeles when there was a switch or there were two parallel groups: the European inspired and the Wright inspired. And they did parallel each other. Wright's houses here, of the textured block period, were rather ornate. The postwar period, after the First World War, was a period of austerity. So decoration was out, as was typical for a postwar period.

MSW: So people tended to like the Europeans more than Wright?

EM: Yes. They felt that was the cheap way to build, and in step with the economy.

MSW: I see. So is Soriano's style a little bit different from Ain's?

EM: Oh, very. Soriano develops a universal space, not the closed room that Neutra did. Neutra was much more private.

MSW: Than Soriano?

EM: Yes. It's like saying that Neutra had secrets, Ain had few, and Soriano is the most open of all. Soriano really was a technician, he even made his own shop drawings. It's too bad that he couldn't work with developers so his houses could be built as tracts. But there were many things he would not give up because he thought they were absolutely necessary—the amenities and the aesthetics.

MSW: Before leaving this second generation, you mention that in 1937 modernism in California changed, and after the 1940s it becomes something else. Is there any reason for the specific dates?

EM: The International Style was not popular in Los Angeles. The change came in order to reach a wider audience. And I think this was important, especially to Neutra. His work softened.

MSW: Do you see some change among the architects in the period of 1937 to 1940?

EM: Yes, yes. I think one reason is that the sun really needed more overhang than the strict International Style would allow, not just a sheer face. And the appeal was greater.

MSW: Before we finish, I would like to get some very general comments from you about why modernism came to Los Angeles from Europe, flowered here in this city, and survived through this period. In the early 1920s or 1930s, even on the East Coast, there were not many modernists, except perhaps [William] Lescaze. But in Los Angeles a lot of modernists gathered together and they survived. Do you see any reason for this?

EM: I think it's the population growth, and also Los Angeles has always been open to new ideas. Los Angeles is not rigid at all. It's a plunger city. San Francisco from the beginning was more oriented to New York and Europe than Los Angeles. So Los Angeles became a place where experimentation was freer. It's true even in postmodernism that Los Angeles has led the way.

—From an interview with Esther McCoy by Makoto Shin Watanabe, *Space Design Magazine*, Kajima Institute Publishing Co., Ltd., Tokyo, Japan, March 1984.

About the MAK Center for Art and Architecture, Los Angeles, at the Schindler House

Acting as a "think tank," the MAK Center for Art and Architecture encourages the exploration of experimental, theoretical, and practical trajectories of contemporary art, architecture, urbanism, design, and international discourse. Offering a year-round schedule of exhibitions, lectures, symposia, public art projects, and concerts, the MAK Center presents programming that challenges conventional notions of architectural space and relationships between the creative arts, thereby making a unique contribution to the artistic and cultural landscape of Los Angeles.

The MAK Center for Art and Architecture, Los Angeles, was founded in 1994 as a satellite of the MAK – Austrian Museum of Applied Arts / Contemporary Art by Peter Noever (1986–2011 CEO and Artistic Director MAK Vienna) in cooperation with the Friends of the Schindler House. The MAK Center's activities are based in three of the most important houses designed by Austrian American visionary architect Rudolph M. Schindler (1887–1953) in West Hollywood and Los Angeles.

The Schindler House, R.M. Schindler's own live-work space built on Kings Road in 1921–22, serves as the public forum for MAK Center activities. A social idealist and experimental architect, Schindler developed a unique approach to design made possible by the moderate California climate. Schindler's ideas about space and the interplay between architecture and landscape were precursors to a new, distinctly Californian conception of architecture. Schindler and his wife Pauline regularly hosted artists, musicians, poets, writers, and actors, turning their West Hollywood home into an axis for avant-garde art and ideas. Today, the Schindler House remains a site for progressive cultural inquiry. It is one of the most beloved architectural and cultural landmarks in Los Angeles. The MAK Center seeks to promote the house and its grounds, as well as its legacy, by working in partnership with the Friends of the Schindler House, a nonprofit organization whose mission is to conserve and maintain the Kings Road house.

Built by Schindler in 1939, the Pearl M. Mackey Apartments were secured by the Republic of Austria in 1994. Soon thereafter, they were established as the location of the first permanent arts residency scholarship program for Austrian artists and architecture students outside of the country. Since then, the Mackey Apartments have become the vibrant base of the MAK Center Artists and Architects in Residence Program, today one of the most sought-after international scholarships. In 2010, the MAK Center completed restoration of the Mackey Apartment garages and construction of the new Garage Top, an exhibition and workspace for the residents and various projects.

The Fitzpatrick-Leland House, built by Schindler in 1936, is an exemplary modern residence located in Los Angeles at the crest of Laurel Canyon Boulevard and Mulholland Drive. The house was donated to the MAK Center by Russ Leland in 2008. Recognizing that the home's light-filled spaces and expansive grounds provide an ideal setting for a residency program, the MAK Center has dedicated the Fitzpatrick-Leland House to the lodging of cultural thinkers, including the MAK Urban Future Initiative Fellows. It serves as an active hub for research, contemplation, and conversation about urban space.

For more information, please visit MAKcenter.org.

Schindler House (R.M. Schindler, 1922)

Fitzpatrick-Leland House
(R.M. Schindler, 1936)

Pearl M. Mackey Apartments
(R.M. Schindler, 1939)

About the MAK Vienna: MAK – Austrian Museum of Applied Arts / Contemporary Art

The MAK regards itself as a laboratory of artistic production at the inter-section of art, architecture and design. With an extraordinary collection of applied and contemporary art, as well as innovative exhibitions, the MAK serves a dual purpose as a conservator of significant objects, and as a center for the scientific research of art with a special emphasis on its on-site production, preservation, and reorientation.

Founded in 1864 as the Imperial and Royal Austrian Museum of Art and Industry, the MAK has pursued a continued commitment to combining practice and theory, art and industry, production and reproduction. The School of Applied Arts, originally an outgrowth of the museum, was later developed into an independent institution, known today as the University of Applied Arts. Under the visionary leadership of Peter Noever, designer and the MAK's long-term director (1986–2011), the museum's original purpose was reconfirmed and radically expanded. The MAK underwent a period of renowned transformation that included the renovation and remodeling of the permanent collection's presentation in a pioneering interplay between artistic heritage and contemporary interventions, as well as the inauguration of one of the two anti-aircraft (flak) towers at Vienna's Arenbergpark as a site for contemporary art.

For more information, please visit MAK.at.

James Turrell, *MAKlite* (2004)
Permanent installation, MAK façade

Artistic intervention by Donald Judd (1993)
MAK Permanent Collection Baroque
Rococo Classicism

Artists in Focus #10, Erwin Wurm
Schöner Wohnen (2011)
Exhibition View
MAK Permanent Collection
Contemporary Art

Photo Credits

Sympathetic Seeing: Esther McCoy and the Heart of American Modernist Architecture and Design is part of Pacific Standard Time. This collaboration, initiated by the Getty, brings together more than sixty cultural institutions from across Southern California for six months beginning October 2011 to tell the story of the birth of the L.A. art scene.

Presenting Sponsors

Sympathetic Seeing is made possible by generous support from:

 GRAHAM FOUNDATION

MAK Center for Art And Architecture, Los Angeles

MAK Center for Art and Architecture
at the Schindler House
835 North Kings Road
West Hollywood, CA 90069
USA

Mackey Apartments
MAK Artists and Architects-in-
Residence Program
1137 South Cochran Avenue
Los Angeles, CA 90019
USA

Fitzpatrick-Leland House
MAK UFI – Urban Future Initiative
8078 Woodrow Wilson Drive
Los Angeles, CA 90046
USA

Tel. (323) 651-1510
Fax (323) 651-2340
Email: office@MAKcenter.org
MAKcenter.org,
MAKcenterUFI.org

DIRECTOR
Kimberli Meyer

MAK GOVERNING COMMITTEE
Michael P. Franz
Harriett F. Gold
Barbara Redl
Robert L. Sweeney
Christoph Thun-Hohenstein
Karin Proidl ex officio

MAK CENTER BOARD OF MEMBERS
Michael P. Franz
Christoph Thun-Hohenstein

MAK CENTER BOARD OF DIRECTORS
Mark Mack
Frederick Samitaur-Smith
Christoph Thun-Hohenstein

MAK Vienna

MAK – Austrian Museum of Applied Arts /
Contemporary Art
Stubenring 5, 1010 Vienna, Austria
Tel. (+43-1) 711 36-0
Fax (+43-1) 713 10 26
Email: office@MAK.at
MAK.at

DIRECTOR and CEO
Christoph Thun-Hohenstein

SUPERVISORY BOARD
Andreas Treichl, Chairman, CEO Erste Bank,
Vienna
Johannes Sereinig, Vice-Chairman,
Vice Chairman of the Managing
Board Verbund
Claudia Biegler, Department of Economic
Affairs of the Vienna School Board
Heinz Hofer-Wittmann, Franz Wittmann
Möbelwerkstätten GmbH
Georg Mayer, MAK
Claudia Oetker, Art Collector,
Frankfurt/Vienna
Wolfgang Polzhuber, Federal Ministry of
Economy, Family and Youth of the
Republic of Austria
August Ruhs, University of Vienna
Alexander Zeuner, Federal Ministry of
Finance of the Republic of Austria